Quilts & Totes for little folks

Welcome a beloved new arrival with cute quilted delights! Three whimsical patterns for crib quilts and coordinating diaper bags are sure to keep Baby cozy and Mommy happy. Splendid sailboats and lively cuddle bugs are versatile in both bold and pastel color schemes, while precious bunnies can be adapted for girls or boys with flower or carrot detailing. Add a playful touch to these charming appliqué and pieced projects with embroidered embellishments. Easy-to-understand instructions and pretty pictures to reference make these childhood charmers go together in no time. So whether you're an expectant mother or a proud friend or relative, you'll have tons of fun creating these quilts and totes for little folks!

Bunny Quilts

Finished Block Size: 12" x 12" (30 cm x 30 cm)
Finished Quilt Size: 37" x 51" (94 cm x 130 cm)

Note: Instructions given are for making a girl bunny quilt, shown on page 2, or a boy bunny quilt, shown on page 6.

YARDAGE REQUIREMENTS

Yardage is based on 45" (114 cm) wide fabric.

- 7/8 yd (80 cm) of background fabric for bunny blocks
- 1/4 yd (23 cm) **each** of 2 contrasting fabrics for pieced blocks
- Scraps of assorted fabrics for appliqués
- 5/8 yd (57 cm) of sashing and inner border fabric
- 1 1/2 yds (1.4 m) of outer border fabric
- 3 3/8 yds (3.1 m) of fabric for backing
- 45" x 59" (1.1 m x 1.5 m) batting
- 3/8 yd (34 cm) of fabric for binding

You will also need:

- Paper-backed fusible web
- Tracing paper
- Transfer paper
- Stabilizer
- Embroidery floss — Black or dark grey for bunnies and assorted colors for other embroidery (You may also use 4mm silk ribbon for flowers and leaves.)
- 7 mm blue silk ribbon for bird's wing on girl bunny
- Four 1/2" diameter (12.7 mm) buttons for boy bunny

CUTTING OUT THE BLOCKS AND BORDERS

*Follow **Rotary Cutting**, page 32, to cut fabric. All measurements include a 1/4" seam allowance. Cutting lengths given for inner borders are exact. You may wish to add an extra 2" of length at each end for "insurance," trimming borders to fit quilt top center. Measurements for background squares include an extra 2". Trim to correct size after appliquéing.*

From background fabric:

- Cut 2 strips 14 1/2" wide. From these strips, cut 3 squares (**A**) 14 1/2" x 14 1/2".

From each of 2 contrasting fabrics:

- Cut 2 strips (**B**) 3 1/2" wide.

From sashing and inner border fabric:

- Cut 3 sashing strips (**C**) 2 1/2" x 12 1/2".
- Cut 2 sashing strips (**D**) 2 1/2" x 26 1/2".
- Cut 2 inner side borders (**E**) 2 1/2" x 40 1/2".
- Cut 2 inner top/bottom borders (**F**) 2 1/2" x 30 1/2".

From outer border fabric:

- Cut 2 lengthwise side borders (**G**) 3 1/2" x 53".
- Cut 2 lengthwise top/bottom borders (**H**) 3 1/2" x 39".

From binding fabric:

- Cut 5 strips 2 1/2" wide.

CUTTING OUT THE APPLIQUÉS

*Appliqué patterns, page 7, do not include seam allowances and are reversed. Follow **Preparing Fusible Appliqué Pieces**, page 34, to cut out appliqués. To help keep blocks organized, lay out all appliqué pieces with corresponding backgrounds as you cut.*

From assorted fabrics:

For boy bunny:

- Cut 3 feet (**a**).
- Cut 1 arm; cut 2 in reverse (**b**).
- Cut 3 arms (**c**).
- Cut 3 bodies (**d**).
- Cut 1 head; cut 2 in reverse (**e**).
- Cut 11 carrots (**f**).
- Cut 1 tail (**g**).

For girl bunny:

- Cut 3 feet (**a**).
- Cut 1 arm (**b**).
- Cut 5 arms (**c**).
- Cut 3 bodies (**d**).
- Cut 1 head; cut 2 in reverse (**e**).
- Cut 1 tail (**g**).
- Cut 1 bird (**h**).

MAKING THE BLOCKS

*Follow **Piecing and Pressing**, page 33, and **Machine Appliqué**, page 34, to make blocks. Refer to photos for placement.*

Block A

1. Alternating colors, sew 4 strips (**B**) together as shown to make **Strip Set**. Cut across **Strip Set** at $3^1/_2$" intervals as shown to make **Unit 1**. Make 12 **Unit 1's**.

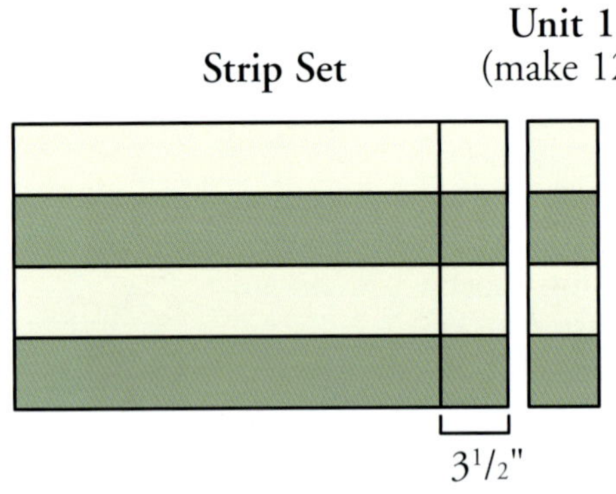

2. Sew 4 **Unit 1's** together as shown to make **Block A**. Make 3 **Block A's**.

Block A Diagram
(make 3)

Blocks B1, B2, and B3

1. Refer to photo for placement of pieces on the 3 bunny blocks. Working in alphabetical order, position pieces (**a-h**) and fuse in place on background squares (**A**).
2. Appliqué pieces in place with a machine Blanket Stitch, using black thread for boy and dark grey thread for girl, to make **Blocks B1**, **B2**, and **B3**. Trim each block to measure $12^1/_2$" x $12^1/_2$".
3. For embellishments, trace embroidered details (shown in blue on patterns) onto tracing paper and transfer markings to fabric pieces.

   For bunnies:
   - Use 2 strands of embroidery floss and a Straight Stitch to stitch nose and mouth.
   - Use 8 strands of black or dark grey embroidery floss and a Straight Stitch to stitch eyes.
   - Use 1 strand of black or dark grey embroidery floss and a Straight Stitch to stitch whiskers.
   - Use 2 strands of black or dark grey embroidery floss and a Stem Stitch to stitch leg detail.

   For flowers (girl only), leaves, and grass:
   - Use 3 strands of embroidery floss and a Stem Stitch to stitch flower stems and grass.
   - Use 3 strands of embroidery floss and a Lazy Daisy Stitch to stitch leaves and carrot tops.
   - Use 4 strands of dark grey embroidery floss to make French Knot flower centers.
   - Use 8 strands of embroidery floss and a Lazy Daisy Stitch to stitch flower petals.

   For dragonflies (boy only) and butterflies (girl only):
   - Use 8 strands of black embroidery floss to make French Knot head. Use 1 strand of black floss and a Stem Stitch to stitch antennae. Use 8 strands of black embroidery floss and Stem Stitch to stitch body.
   - For dragonflies, use 4 strands of embroidery floss and a Lazy Daisy Stitch to stitch wings.
   - For butterfly, use 6 strands of embroidery floss and a Lazy Daisy Stitch to stitch wings.

   For bird (girl only):
   - Use blue silk ribbon and Lazy Daisy Stitch to stitch wing and Straight Stitch to stitch tail.
   - Use 2 strands of embroidery floss and a Straight Stitch to stitch eye and beak.

ASSEMBLING THE QUILT TOP

Refer to photo to make the quilt top.

1. Sew 1 **Block A**, 1 **Block B1**, **B2**, or **B3**, and 1 **Sashing Strip** (**C**) together as shown to make **Rows 1-3**.
2. Sew **Rows 1-3** and 2 **Sashing Strips** (**D**) together as shown to make **Quilt Top Center**.

ADDING THE BORDERS

Inner Border

1. Measure **Quilt Top Center** and trim borders to length if necessary.
2. Matching centers and corners and easing in fullness, sew inner side borders (**E**), then inner top/bottom borders (**F**) to **Quilt Top Center**.

Outer Border

1. Refer to **Adding Mitered Borders**, page 35, to sew outer side borders (**G**), then outer top/bottom borders (**H**) to pieced center to make quilt top.

COMPLETING THE QUILT

1. Follow **Quilting**, page 36, to mark, layer, and quilt as desired. Our quilt was outline quilted by hand around the appliqués and machine quilted "in the ditch" around blocks and borders.
2. Follow **Making Straight Grain Binding**, page 38, to make $5^1/_4$ yds of $2^1/_2$"w binding.
3. Follow **Attaching Binding with Mitered Corners,** page 38, to attach binding to quilt.
4. Sew 2 buttons to boy bunny. **Note:** Because they present a choking hazard for babies and small children, you may want to omit the buttons.

Quilt Top Diagram

Boy Bunny Quilt

Bunny Patterns

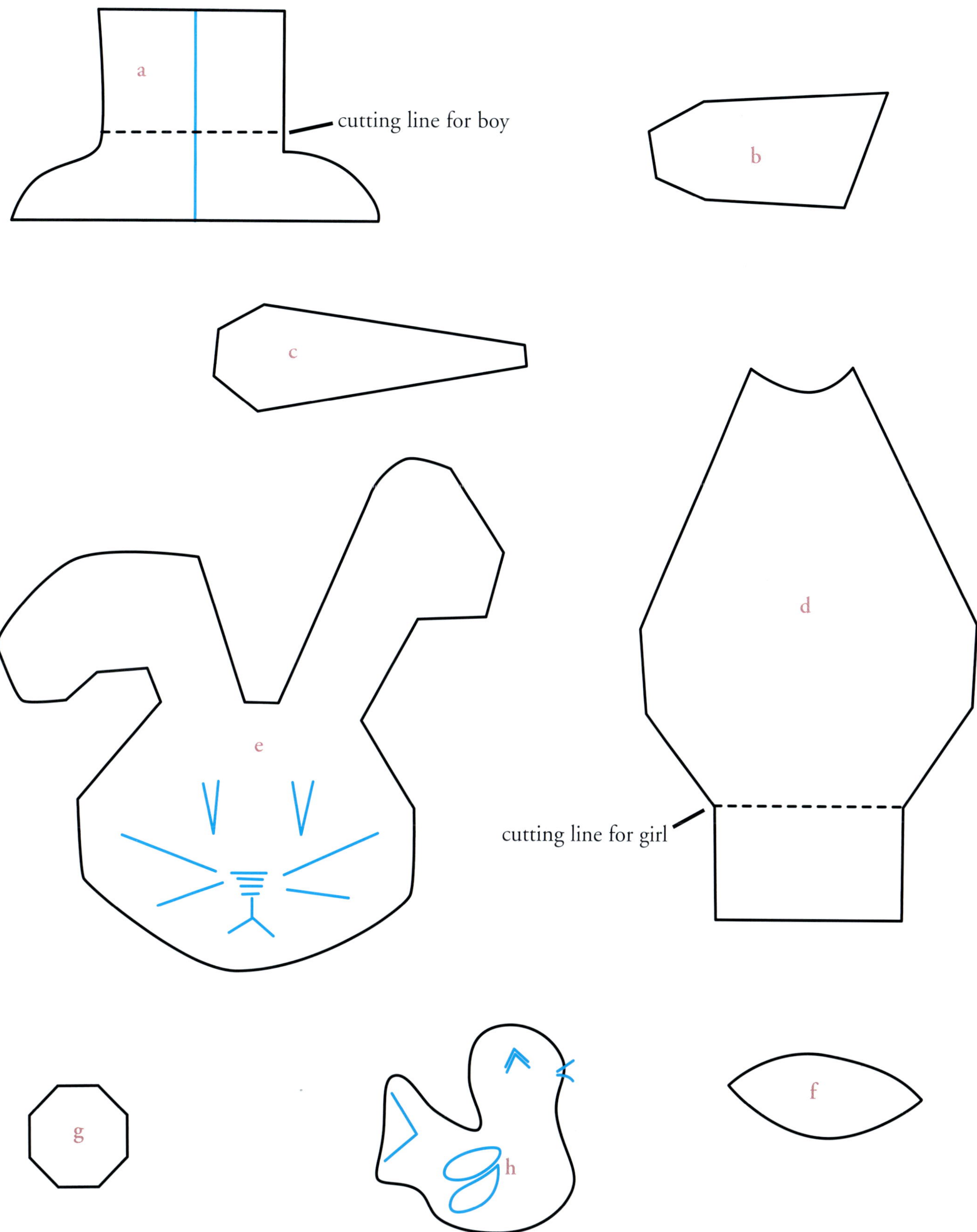

Bunny Diaper Tote

FABRIC REQUIREMENTS

Yardage is based on 45" (114 cm) wide fabric.

1$^{3}/_{8}$ yds (1.3 m) of fabric for tote and pocket
1$^{3}/_{8}$ yds (1.3 m) **total** of 2 contrasting fabrics for lining and pocket trim, binding, and bottom
Scraps of assorted fabrics for appliqués
32" x 47" (81 cm x 119 cm) rectangle of batting

You will also need:

Paper-backed fusible web
Tracing paper
Transfer paper
Stabilizer
Embroidery floss — Black or dark grey for bunnies and assorted colors for other embroidery (You may also use 4mm silk ribbon for flowers and leaves)
Two $^{1}/_{2}$" diameter (12.7 mm) buttons for boy bunny

CUTTING OUT THE PIECES

*Follow **Rotary Cutting**, page 32, to cut fabric. Measurements include a $^{1}/_{2}$" seam allowance unless otherwise noted. Appliqué patterns, page 7, do not include seam allowances and are reversed. Follow **Preparing Fusible Appliqué Pieces**, page 34, to cut out appliqués from assorted fabrics.*

From tote fabric:

- Cut 1 rectangle 15" x 45" for tote and 1 rectangle 15" x 13" for pocket.

From 2 contrasting fabrics:

- Cut 1 rectangle 15" x 45". Fold rectangle in half lengthwise and crosswise and referring to **Fig. 1**, page 29, use **Template**, page 29, to cut tote lining.
- Cut 1 rectangle 15" x 2$^{1}/_{2}$" for pocket binding.
- Cut 1 rectangle 15" x 13" for pocket lining.
- Cut 2 rectangles 15" x 3$^{1}/_{2}$" for tote bottom.
- For boy's tote, cut 2 rectangles 15" x 1$^{1}/_{2}$" for pocket trim.

From assorted fabrics for appliqués:

For **each** bunny:

- Cut 1 foot (**a**).
- Cut 1 arm (**b**).
- Cut 1 arm (**c**).
- Cut 1 body (**d**).
- Cut 1 head (**e**).

For boy bunny only:

- Cut 3 carrots (**f**).

From batting:

- Cut 1 rectangle 15" x 45" for tote.
- Cut 1 rectangle 15" x 13" for pocket.

MAKING THE TOTE

*Follow **Piecing** and **Pressing**, page 33, to make tote. Refer to photo for placement. Use a $^{1}/_{2}$" seam allowance for all seams, unless otherwise noted.*

1. Center bunny pieces horizontally on tote pocket, allowing a 1" margin at the top edge and a 3$^{1}/_{2}$" margin at the bottom edge. Working in alphabetical order, fuse pieces on pocket and appliqué in place with a machine Blanket Stitch, using black thread for boy bunny and dark grey thread for girl bunny.
2. Refer to Bunny Quilt, Making the Blocks, Step 3, to add embroidered details to the bunny and background.
3. Refer to **Diaper Tote Finishing**, page 40, to assemble the tote.
4. For squared bottom, match side seams of tote to center bottom seam; sew across each corner 2" from end (**Fig. 2**). Repeat for lining.

Fig. 2

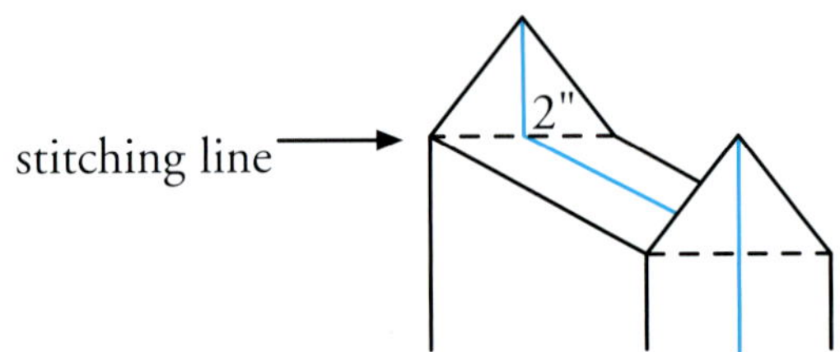

5. Turn right side out and blindstitch opening in lining closed. Place lining inside tote and press.

Girl Bunny Diaper Tote

Boy Bunny Diaper Tote

CUDDLE
BUGS

Cuddle Bugs Quilt
Version 1

Finished Size: 40 1/2" x 49 1/2" (103 cm x 126 cm)

YARDAGE REQUIREMENTS

Yardage is based on 45" (114 cm) wide fabric.

- 3/4 yd (69 cm) of white print fabric for blocks and borders
- 1 5/8 yds (1.5 m) of floral print fabric for appliqués, blocks, and outer borders
- 1 5/8 yds (1.5 m) of light print fabric for appliqués, blocks, and inner borders
- 1/2 yd (46 cm) of medium print fabric
- Scraps of assorted fabrics for appliqués
- 3 1/4 yds (3.0 m) of fabric for backing
- 49" x 58" (1.2 m x 1.5 m) batting
- 1/2 yd (46 cm) of fabric for binding

You will also need:

- Paper-backed fusible web
- Tracing paper
- Transfer paper
- Stabilizer
- Embroidery floss — black for both versions and yellow, white, and light green for Version 2 (You may also use 4 mm silk ribbon for the leaves.)

CUTTING OUT THE BLOCKS AND BORDERS

*Follow **Rotary Cutting**, page 32, to cut fabric. All measurements include a 1/4" seam allowance.*

From white print fabric:

- Cut 1 strip (**A**) 1 1/2" x 26".
- Cut 2 inner side borders (**B**) 1 1/2" x 35".
- Cut 2 inner top/bottom borders (**C**) 1 1/2" x 28".
- Cut 1 strip 3 1/2" wide. From this strip, cut 1 rectangle (**D**) 3 1/2" x 27" and 1 square (**E**) 3 1/2" x 3 1/2".
- Cut 1 strip 9 1/2" wide. From this strip, cut 1 background square (**F**) 9 1/2" x 9 1/2".

From floral print fabric:

- Cut 2 lengthwise outer side borders (**G**) 3" x 51".
- Cut 2 lengthwise outer top/bottom borders (**H**) 3" x 42".

From remaining width:

- Cut 2 strips 3 1/2" wide. From these strips, cut 1 rectangle (**I**) 3 1/2" x 27" and 2 squares (**J**) 3 1/2" x 3 1/2".
- Cut 1 square 15" x 15". Cut square twice diagonally to make 4 triangles (**K**).

From light print fabric:

- Cut 2 lengthwise middle side borders (**L**) 4" x 51".
- Cut 2 lengthwise middle top/bottom borders (**M**) 4" x 42".

From remaining width:

- Cut 1 rectangle (**N**) 3 1/2" x 27".

From medium print fabric:

- Cut 1 strip 15" wide. From this strip, cut 1 square 15" x 15". Cut square twice diagonally to make 4 triangles (**O**).

From remaining width:

- Cut 1 background rectangle (**P**) 8 1/2" x 26".

From binding fabric:

- Cut 5 strips 2 1/2" wide.

CUTTING OUT THE APPLIQUÉS

*Appliqué patterns, page 17, do not include seam allowances and are reversed. Follow **Preparing Fusible Appliqué Pieces**, page 34, to cut out appliqués.*

Cuddle Bugs Version 1

From assorted fabrics:

- Cut 2 dragonfly wings (**a**).
- Cut 2 dragonfly wings (**b**).
- Cut 2 dragonfly bodies (**c**).
- Cut 1 butterfly wing (**d**).
- Cut 1 butterfly wing (**e**).
- Cut 1 butterfly body (**f**).
- Cut 6 bee wings (**g**).
- Cut 3 bee bodies (**h**).
- Cut 3 bee heads (**i**).
- Cut 4 bug bodies (**j**).
- Cut 4 bug wings (**k**).
- Use **Alphabet**, pages 30-31, to cut letters.

Cuddle Bugs Version 2

From assorted fabrics:

- Cut 2 dragonfly wings (**a**).
- Cut 2 dragonfly wings (**b**).
- Cut 2 dragonfly bodies (**c**).
- Cut 2 butterfly wings (**d**).
- Cut 2 butterfly wings (**e**).
- Cut 2 butterfly bodies (**f**).
- Cut 5 bug bodies (**j**).
- Cut 5 bug wings (**k**).
- Use **Alphabet**, pages 30-31, to cut letters for name.

MAKING THE BLOCKS

*Follow **Piecing and Pressing**, page 33, to make blocks. Working in alphabetical order, refer to **Quilt Top Diagram**, page 14, and photos, page 10 or 15, for placement of appliqués.*

Blocks A and B

1. Sew 1 white print rectangle (**D**), 1 floral print rectangle (**I**), and 1 light print rectangle (**N**) together as shown to make **Strip Set A**. Cut across **Strip Set A** twice at $3^1/_2$" intervals and twice at $9^1/_2$" intervals as shown to make 2 **Unit 1's** and 2 **Block A's**.

Strip Set A

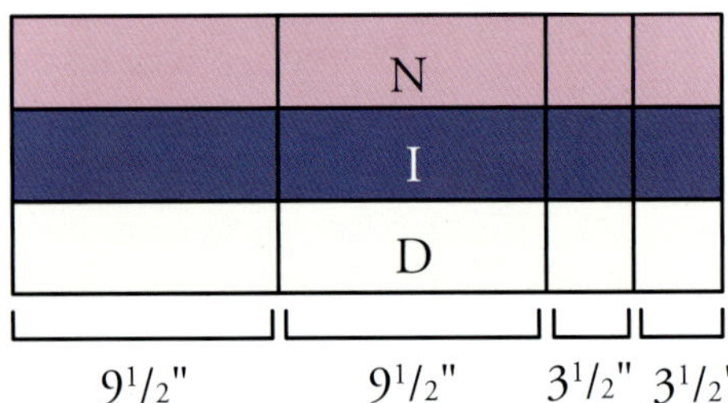

Unit 1
(make 2)

Block A Diagram
(make 2)

2. Sew 1 white print square (**E**) and 2 floral print squares (**J**) together as shown to make **Unit 2**.

Unit 2

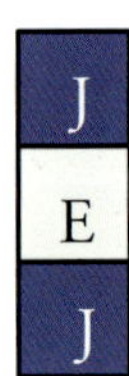

3. Sew 2 **Unit 1's** and 1 **Unit 2** together as shown to make **Block B**.

Block B Diagram

ASSEMBLING THE QUILT TOP

*Refer to **Quilt Top Diagram** to make the quilt top.*

1. Sew 2 **Block A's**, **Block B**, and white print square (**F**) together as shown to make **Unit 3**.

Unit 3

2. Sew a floral print triangle (**K**) and a medium print triangle (**O**) together as shown to make **Unit 4**. Make 2 **Unit 4's**.

Unit 4
(make 2)

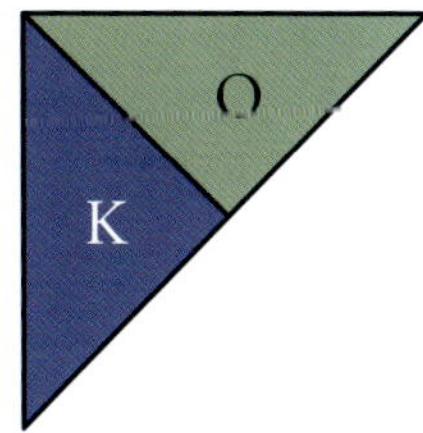

3. Sew a floral print triangle (**K**) and a medium print triangle (**O**) together as shown to make **Unit 5**. Make 2 **Unit 5's**.

Unit 5
(make 2)

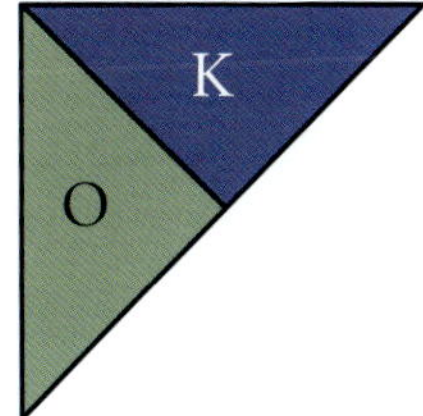

4. Sew 2 **Unit 4's** and 2 **Unit 5's** to **Unit 3** as shown to make **Unit 6**. Trim **Unit 6** to measure 26" x 26".

Unit 6

5. Sew **Unit 6**, white print strip (**A**), and medium print rectangle (**P**) together as shown to make **Quilt Top Center**.
6. Fuse butterfly to center of white print square. For Version 1, fuse dragonflies, bugs, bees, and "CUDDLE BUGS" on **Quilt Top Center** as desired. For Version 2, fuse butterfly, dragonflies, bugs, and name on **Quilt Top Center** as desired. Follow **Machine Appliqué** page 34, to appliqué pieces in place using black thread and a machine Blanket Stitch.
7. For embellishments, trace embroidered details (shown in blue on patterns) onto tracing paper and transfer markings to fabric pieces.
   For bees, bugs, dragonflies, and butterflies:
   - Use 2 strands of black embroidery floss and a Stem Stitch to stitch antennae.
   - Use 2 strands of black embroidery floss to add a French Knot to end of antennae.
   - Use 4 strands of black embroidery floss and a Stem Stitch to add lines to bees' bodies and bugs' wings.
   - Use 4 strands of black embroidery floss and a French Knot to make spots on bugs.

   For flowers (Version 2):
   - Use 4 strands of white or yellow embroidery floss and a Lazy Daisy Stitch to stitch flower petals as desired.
   - Use 4 strands of black embroidery floss for French Knot centers.
   - Use 4 strands of green embroidery floss and a Lazy Daisy Stitch to stitch leaves.

ADDING THE BORDERS

*Refer to **Quilt Top Diagram** to add the borders.*

1. Sew inner side borders (**B**), then inner top/bottom borders (**C**) to **Quilt Top Center.**
2. Matching centers, sew middle side borders (**L**) and outer side borders (**G**) together to make 2 **Side Border Units.** Repeat for middle top/bottom borders (**M**) and outer top/bottom borders (**H**) to make 2 **Top/Bottom Border Units.**
3. Refer to **Adding Mitered Borders**, page 35, to sew **Side Border Units** and **Top/Bottom Border Units** to pieced center to make quilt top.

COMPLETING THE QUILT

1. Follow **Quilting**, page 36, to mark, layer, and quilt as desired. Our quilt was outline quilted by hand around the appliqués and machine quilted "in the ditch" around blocks and borders.
2. Follow **Making Straight Grain Binding**, page 38, to make 5³/₈ yds of 2¹/₂"w binding.
3. Follow **Attaching Binding with Mitered Corners**, page 38, to attach binding to quilt.

Quilt Top Diagram

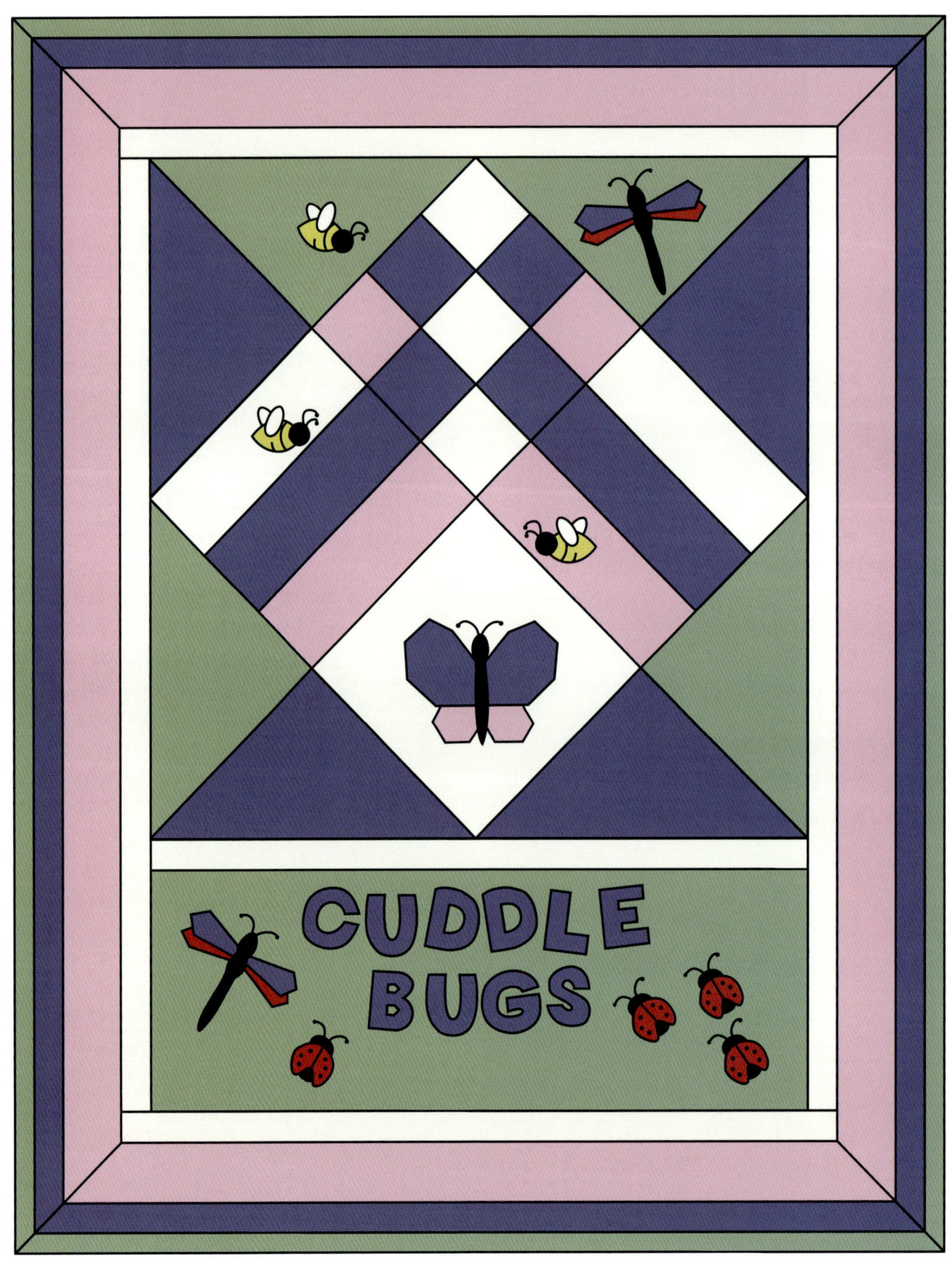

Cuddle Bugs Quilt
version 2

Cuddle Bugs Diaper Tote

FABRIC REQUIREMENTS

Yardage is based on 45" (114 cm) wide fabric.

1 yd (91 cm) of fabric for tote and pocket
1 yd (91 cm) **total** of 2 contrasting fabrics for lining and pocket trim, binding, and bottom
Scraps of assorted fabrics for appliqués
1 yd (91 cm) of batting

You will also need:

Paper-backed fusible web
Tracing paper
Transfer paper
Stabilizer
Embroidery floss — black
Two 3" (7.6 cm) lengths of 1/2" (1.3 cm) wide lace

CUTTING OUT THE PIECES

*Follow **Rotary Cutting**, page 32, to cut fabric. All measurements include a 1/2" seam allowance. Appliqué patterns do not include seam allowances and are reversed. Follow **Preparing Fusible Appliqué Pieces**, page 34, to cut out appliqués.*

From tote fabric:

- Cut 2 strips 15" wide. From these strips, cut 1 rectangle 15" x 43" for tote and 1 rectangle 15" x 13" for pocket.

From 2 contrasting fabrics:

- Cut 1 strip 15" wide. Fold strip in half lengthwise and crosswise and use **Template**, page 29, to cut tote lining.
- Cut 1 rectangle 15" x 2 1/2" for pocket binding.
- Cut 1 rectangle 15" x 13" for pocket lining.
- Cut 2 rectangles 15" x 3 1/2" for tote bottom.
- Cut 2 rectangles 15" x 1 1/2" for pocket trim.

From assorted fabrics for appliques:

- Cut 1 butterfly wing (**d**).
- Cut 1 butterfly wing (**e**).
- Cut 1 butterfly body (**f**).
- Cut 1 bee body (**h**).
- Cut 1 bee head (**i**).

From batting:

- Cut 1 rectangle 15" x 43" for tote.
- Cut 1 rectangle 15" x 13" for pocket.

MAKING THE TOTE

*Follow **Piecing and Pressing**, page 33, and **Machine Appliqué**, page 34, to make tote. Refer to photo for placement. Use a 1/2" seam allowance for all seams.*

1. Position appliqués on tote pocket, allowing a 1" margin at the top edge and a 3 1/2" margin at the bottom edge. For bee wings, match cut ends and fold lace in half, forming a point (**Fig. 1**). Position cut ends of wings under bee body before appliquéing. Working in alphabetical order, fuse pieces in place on pocket. Appliqué in place using black thread and a machine Blanket Stitch.

Fig. 1

2. For embellishments, trace embroidered details (shown in blue on patterns) onto tracing paper and transfer markings to fabric pieces.
   - Use 2 strands of black embroidery floss and a Stem Stitch to stitch antennae.
   - Use 2 strands of black embroidery floss to add a French Knot to end of antennae.
   - Use 4 strands of black embroidery floss and a Stem Stitch to add lines to bee.
3. Refer to **Diaper Tote Finishing**, page 40, to complete the tote.

Cuddle Bug Patterns

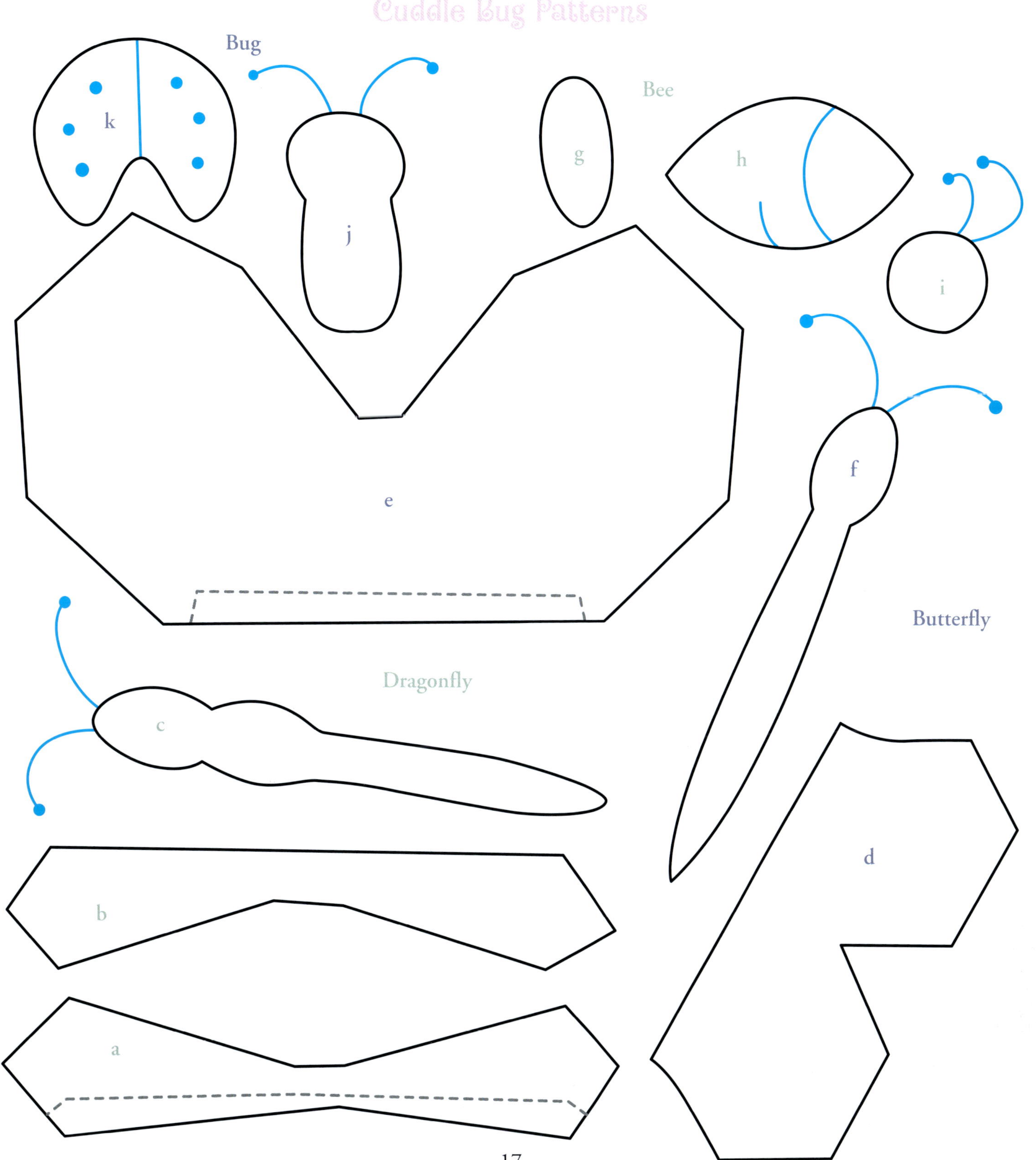

AHOY!

Sailboat Quilt

Version 1

Finished Block Size: $7\frac{1}{2}$" x $7\frac{1}{2}$" (19 cm x 19 cm)
Finished Size: $38\frac{1}{2}$" x $53\frac{1}{2}$" (98 cm x 136 cm)

YARDAGE REQUIREMENTS

Yardage is based on 45" (114 cm) wide fabric.

- $\frac{5}{8}$ yd (57 cm) of blue solid fabric for sailboat blocks
- 1yd (91 cm) **each** of white and multicolor print fabrics
- $\frac{7}{8}$ yd (80 cm) of yellow print fabric
- Scraps of assorted fabrics for sails and appliqués
- $3\frac{1}{2}$ yds (3.2 m) of fabric for backing
- 47" x 62" (1.2 m x 1.6 m) batting
- $\frac{3}{8}$ yd (34 cm) of fabric for binding

You will also need:

- Fusible Interfacing
- Paper-backed fusible web
- Stabilizer
- Six 7" (18 cm) lengths of $\frac{3}{8}$" (.95 cm) wide grosgrain ribbon

CUTTING OUT THE BLOCKS AND BORDERS

*Follow **Rotary Cutting**, page 32, to cut fabric. All measurements include a $\frac{1}{4}$" seam allowance. Measurements for background squares include an extra 2". Trim to correct size after appliquéing.*

From blue solid fabric:

- Cut 2 strips 10" wide. From these strips, cut 6 background squares (**A**) 10" x 10".

From multicolor print fabric:

- Cut 9 strips (**B**) 3" x 26".
- Cut 4 strips (**C**) 3" x 20".

From white print fabric:

- Cut 9 strips (**D**) 3" x 26".
- Cut 2 strips (**E**) 3" x 20".

From yellow print fabric:

- Cut 9 strips (**F**) 3" x 26".

From binding fabric:

- Cut 5 strips $2\frac{1}{2}$" wide.

CUTTING OUT THE APPLIQUÉS

*Appliqué patterns, page 28, do not include seam allowances and are reversed. Follow **Preparing Fusible Appliqué Pieces**, page 34, to cut out appliqués. To help keep blocks organized, lay out all appliqué pieces with corresponding backgrounds as you cut.*

From assorted fabrics:

- Cut 6 boats (**a**).
- Cut 6 sails (**b**).
- Cut 6 sails (**c**).

MAKING THE BLOCKS

*Follow **Piecing** and **Pressing**, page 33, and **Machine Appliqué**, page 34, to make blocks. Refer to **Block Diagrams**, page 20, and photo for placement. **Note:** We used a Satin Stitch to attach appliqués.*

Block A

1. Sew 1 white print strip (**D**), 1 multicolor print strip (**B**), and 1 yellow print strip (**F**) together as shown to make **Strip Set A**. Make 9 **Strip Set A's**. Cut across 6 **Strip Set A's** at 8" intervals to make **Block A**. Make 17 **Block A's**.

Strip Set A
(make 9)

F
B
D

Block A Diagram
(make 17)

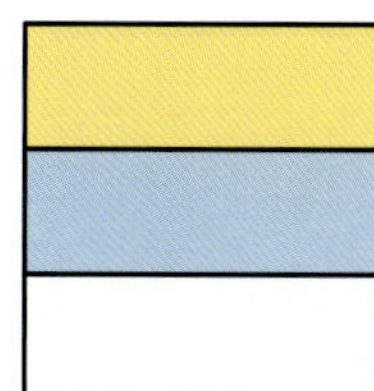

Block B

1. Cut across 3 remaining **Strip Set A's** at 3" intervals to make **Unit 1**. Make 24 **Unit 1's**.

Unit 1
(make 24)

2. Sew 1 white print strip (**E**) and 2 multicolor print strips (**C**) together as shown to make **Strip Set B**. Make 2 **Strip Set B's**. Cut across **Strip Set B's** at 3" intervals as shown to make **Unit 2**. Make 12 **Unit 2's**.

Strip Set B
(make 2)

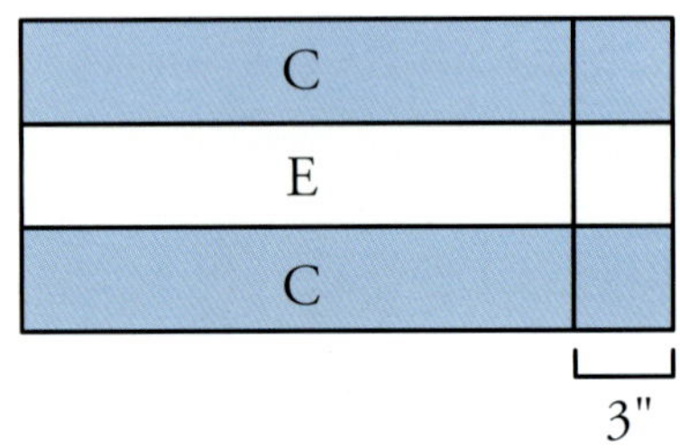

Unit 2
(make 12)

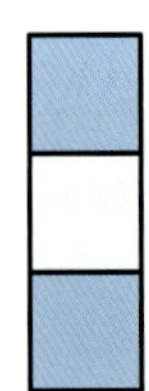

3. Sew 2 **Unit 1's** and 1 **Unit 2** together as shown to make **Block B**. Make 12 **Block B's**.

Block B Diagram
(make 12)

Block C

1. Position sails (**b** and **c**) on background square (**A**) and fuse in place. Appliqué sails in place using matching thread and a Satin Stitch.
2. Position ribbon over center sail seam with bottom of ribbon extending 1" below sails. Trim top end of ribbon diagonally. Fold $1\frac{1}{2}$" of ribbon under as shown in **Fig. 1**. Edge stitch ribbon in place.

Fig. 1

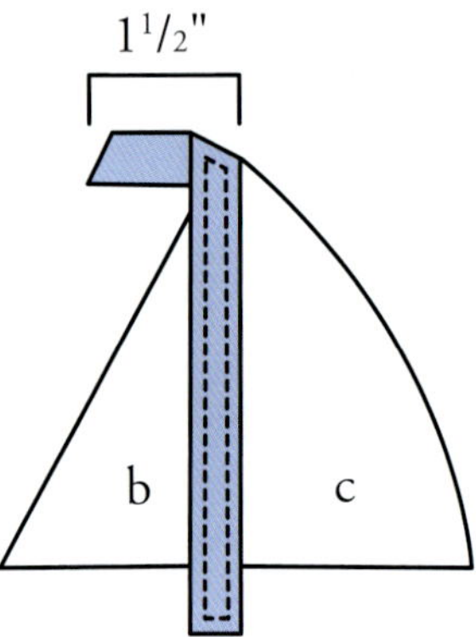

3. Position boat (**a**) over bottom of ribbon. Fuse boat in place and appliqué using matching thread and a Satin Stitch to complete **Block C**. Trim block to measure 8" x 8". Make 6 **Block C's**.

Block C Diagram
(make 6)

ASSEMBLING THE QUILT TOP

*Refer to **Quilt Top Diagram** to make the quilt top.*

1. Sew 2 **Block A's** and 3 **Block B's** together as shown to make **Unit 3**. Make 2 **Unit 3's**.
2. Sew 2 **Block A's** and 3 **Block B's** together as shown to make **Unit 4**. Make 2 **Unit 4's**.
3. Sew 3 **Block A's** and 2 **Block C's** together as shown to make **Unit 5**. Make 2 **Unit 5's**.
4. Sew 3 **Block A's** and 2 **Block C's** together as shown to make **Unit 6**.
5. Sew **Units 3**, **4**, **5**, and **6** together as shown to make **Quilt Top**.

COMPLETING THE QUILT

1. Follow **Quilting**, page 36, to mark, layer, and quilt as desired. Our quilt was outline quilted by hand around the appliqués and machine quilted "in the ditch" around blocks.
2. Follow **Making Straight Grain Binding**, page 38, to make $5^1/_2$ yds of $2^1/_2$"w binding.
3. Follow **Attaching Binding with Mitered Corners**, page 38, to attach binding to quilt.

Quilt Top Diagram

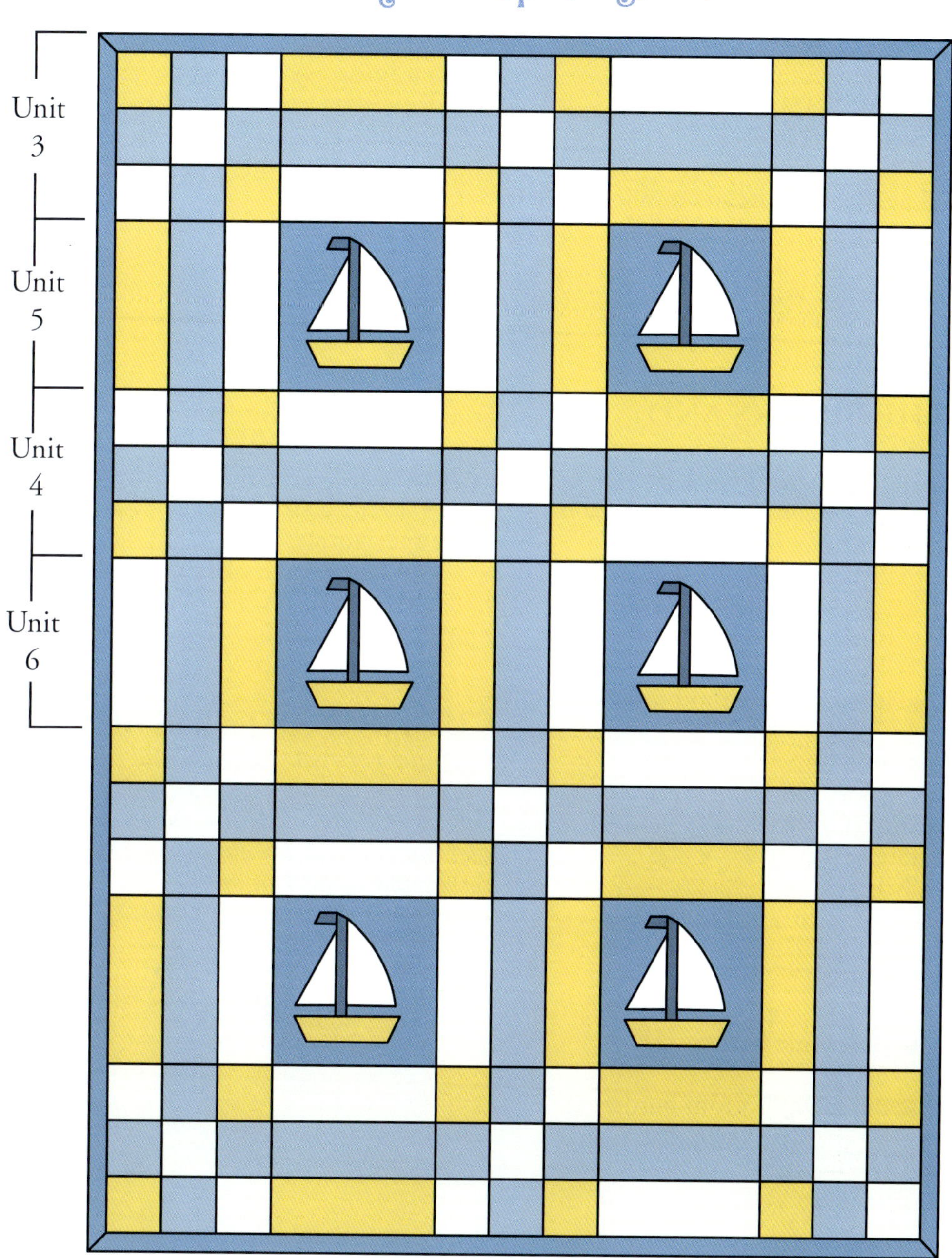

Sailboat Quilt
Version 2

Finished Block Size: 6" x 6" (15 cm x 15 cm)
Finished Size: 39" x 51" (99 cm x 130 cm)

YARDAGE REQUIREMENTS

Yardage is based on 45" (114 cm) wide fabric.
- 1 1/2 yds (1.4 m) of blue solid fabric
- 3/4 yd (69 cm) of multicolor print fabric
- 1 1/2 yds (1.4 m) of red solid fabric
- 3/4 yd (69 cm) of dark blue solid fabric
- Scraps of assorted fabrics for sails and appliqués
- 3 3/8 yds (3.1 m) of fabric for backing
- 47" x 59" (1.2 m x 1.5 m) batting
- 3/8 yd (34 cm) of fabric for binding

You will also need:
- Fusible interfacing
- Paper-backed fusible web
- Stabilizer
- Four 7" (18 cm) lengths of 5/8" (1.6 cm) wide grosgrain ribbon

CUTTING OUT THE BLOCKS AND BORDERS

*Follow **Rotary Cutting**, page 32, to cut fabric. All measurements include a 1/4" seam allowance. Measurements for background squares and rectangles include an extra 2". Trim to correct size after appliquéing.*

From blue solid fabric:
- Cut 2 lengthwise inner side borders (**A**) 2 1/2" x 52".
- Cut 2 lengthwise inner top/bottom borders (**B**) 2 1/2" x 40".

From remaining width:
- Cut 2 strips 8 1/2" wide. From these strips, cut 4 background squares (**C**) 8 1/2" x 8 1/2" and 1 background rectangle (**D**) 20 1/2" x 8 1/2".

From multicolor print fabric:
- Cut 4 strips (**E**) 2 1/2" x 28".
- Cut 3 strips (**F**) 2 1/2" x 22".
- Cut 4 strips (**G**) 2 1/2" x 17".

From red solid fabric:
- Cut 2 lengthwise outer side borders (**H**) 2 1/2" x 52".
- Cut 2 lengthwise outer top/bottom borders (**I**) 2 1/2" x 40".

From remaining width:
- Cut 4 strips (**J**) 2 1/2" x 28".
- Cut 3 strips (**K**) 2 1/2" x 22".

From dark blue solid fabric:
- Cut 4 strips (**L**) 2 1/2" x 28".
- Cut 3 strips (**M**) 2 1/2" x 22".
- Cut 2 strips (**N**) 2 1/2" x 17.".

From sail fabrics:
- Cut 2 **each** of sail, interfacing, and lining; cut 2 **each** in reverse of sail, interfacing, and lining (**e**).

From binding fabric:
- Cut 5 strips 2 1/2" wide.

CUTTING OUT THE APPLIQUÉS

*Appliqué patterns, pages 28 and 30-31, do not include seam allowances and are reversed. Follow **Preparing Fusible Appliqué Pieces**, page 34, to cut out appliqués. To help keep blocks organized, lay out all appliqué pieces with corresponding backgrounds as you cut.*

From assorted fabrics for appliqués:
- Cut 4 boats (**a**).
- Cut 2 sails; cut 2 in reverse (**d**).
- Use **Alphabet**, pages 30-31, to cut letters for name.

ZACHARY

MAKING THE BLOCKS

*Follow **Piecing and Pressing**, page 33, and **Machine Appliqué**, page 34, to make blocks. Refer to **Block Diagrams** and photo, page 23, for placement.*

Block A

1. Sew 1 dark blue solid strip (L), 1 multicolor print strip (E), and 1 red solid strip (J) together as shown to make **Strip Set A**. Make 4 **Strip Set A's**. Cut across **Strip Set A's** at 6 1/2" intervals as shown to make **Block A**. Make 16 **Block A's**.

Strip Set A
(make 4)

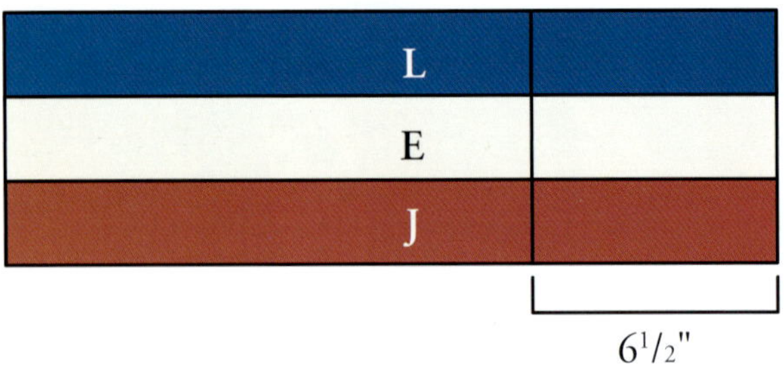

Block A Diagram
(make 16)

Block B

1. Sew 1 blue solid strip (M), 1 multicolor print strip (F), and 1 red solid strip (K) together as shown to make **Strip Set B**. Make 3 **Strip Set B's**. Cut across **Strip Set B's** at 2 1/2" intervals as shown to make **Unit 1**. Make 24 **Unit 1's**.

Strip Set B
(make 3)

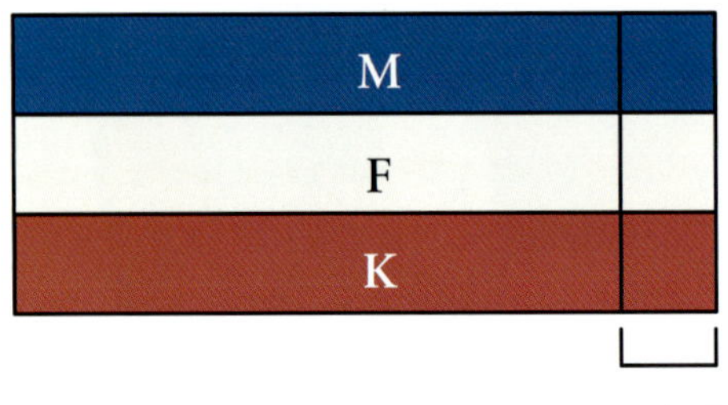

Unit 1
(make 24)

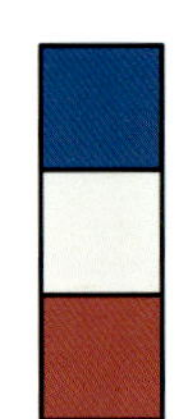

2. Sew 1 dark blue solid strip (N) and 2 multicolor print strips (G) together as shown to make **Strip Set C**. Make 2 **Strip Set C's**. Cut across **Strip Set C's** at 2 1/2" intervals as shown to make **Unit 2**. Make 12 **Unit 2's**.

Strip Set C
(make 2)

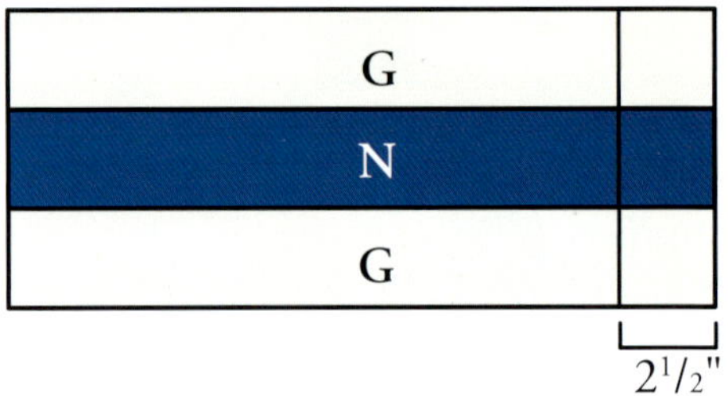

Unit 2
(make 12)

3. Sew 2 **Unit 1's** and 1 **Unit 2** together as shown to make **Block B**. Make 12 **Block B's**.

Block B Diagram
(make 12)

Block C

1. For detached sail, follow manufacturer's instructions to fuse interfacing to wrong side of sail (**e**). Matching right sides and raw edges, sew sail and lining together along bottom and curved edges. Turn right side out and press. Position sail (**e**) on blue solid square (**C**) and baste in place along raw edge.
2. Position sail (**d**) on blue solid square (**C**) and fuse in place. Appliqué sail using dark blue thread and a machine Blanket Stitch.
3. Position ribbon over center sail seam with bottom of ribbon extending 1" below sails. Trim top end of ribbon. Fold $1^1/_2$" of ribbon under as shown in **Fig. 1**. Edge stitch ribbon in place.

Fig. 1

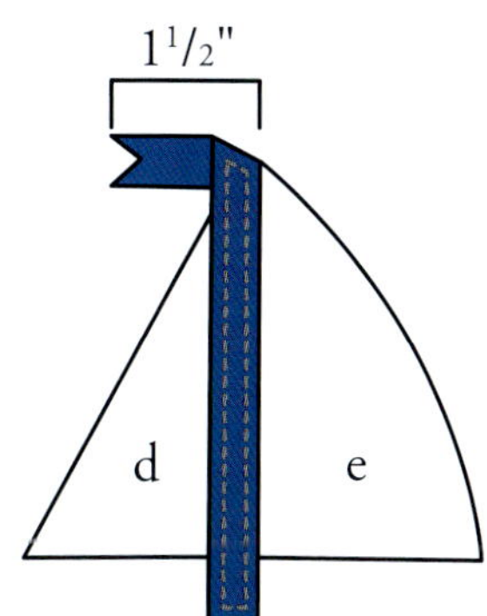

4. Fuse boat (**a**) in place and appliqué using dark blue thread and a machine Blanket Stitch to complete **Block C**. Trim block to measure $6^1/_2$" x $6^1/_2$". Make 4 **Block C's**.

Block C Diagram
(make 4)

Block D

1. Position letters as desired on blue solid rectangle (**D**) and fuse in place. Appliqué letters using dark blue thread and a machine Blanket Stitch to complete **Block D**. Trim block to measure $18^1/_2$" x $6^1/_2$".

ASSEMBLING THE QUILT TOP

Refer to ***Quilt Top Diagram****, page 26, to make the quilt top.*

1. Sew 2 **Block A's** and 3 **Block B's** together as shown to make **Unit 3**. Make 2 **Unit 3's**.
2. Sew 2 **Block A's** and 3 **Block B's** together as shown to make **Unit 4**. Make 2 **Unit 4's**.
3. Sew 3 **Block A's** and 2 **Block C's** together as shown to make **Unit 5**.
4. Sew 3 **Block A's** and 2 **Block C's** together as shown to make **Unit 6**.
5. Sew 2 **Block A's** and **Block D** together as shown to make **Unit 7**.
6. Sew **Units 3**, **4**, **5**, **6**, and **7** together as shown to make **Quilt Top Center**.

ADDING THE BORDERS

1. Matching centers, sew blue inner side borders (**A**) and red outer side borders (**H**) together to make 2 **Side Border Units**. Repeat for blue inner top/bottom borders (**B**) and red outer top/bottom borders (**I**) to make 2 **Top/Bottom Border Units**.
2. Refer to **Adding Mitered Borders**, page 35, to sew **Side** and **Top/Bottom Border Units** to pieced center to make quilt top.

COMPLETING THE QUILT

1. Follow **Quilting**, page 36, to mark, layer, and quilt as desired. Our quilt was hand quilted around the appliqués and machine quilted "in the ditch" around blocks and borders.
2. Follow **Making Straight Grain Binding**, page 38, to make $5^1/_2$ yds of $2^1/_2$"w binding.
3. Follow **Attaching Binding with Mitered Corners**, page 38, to attach binding to quilt.

Quilt Top Diagram

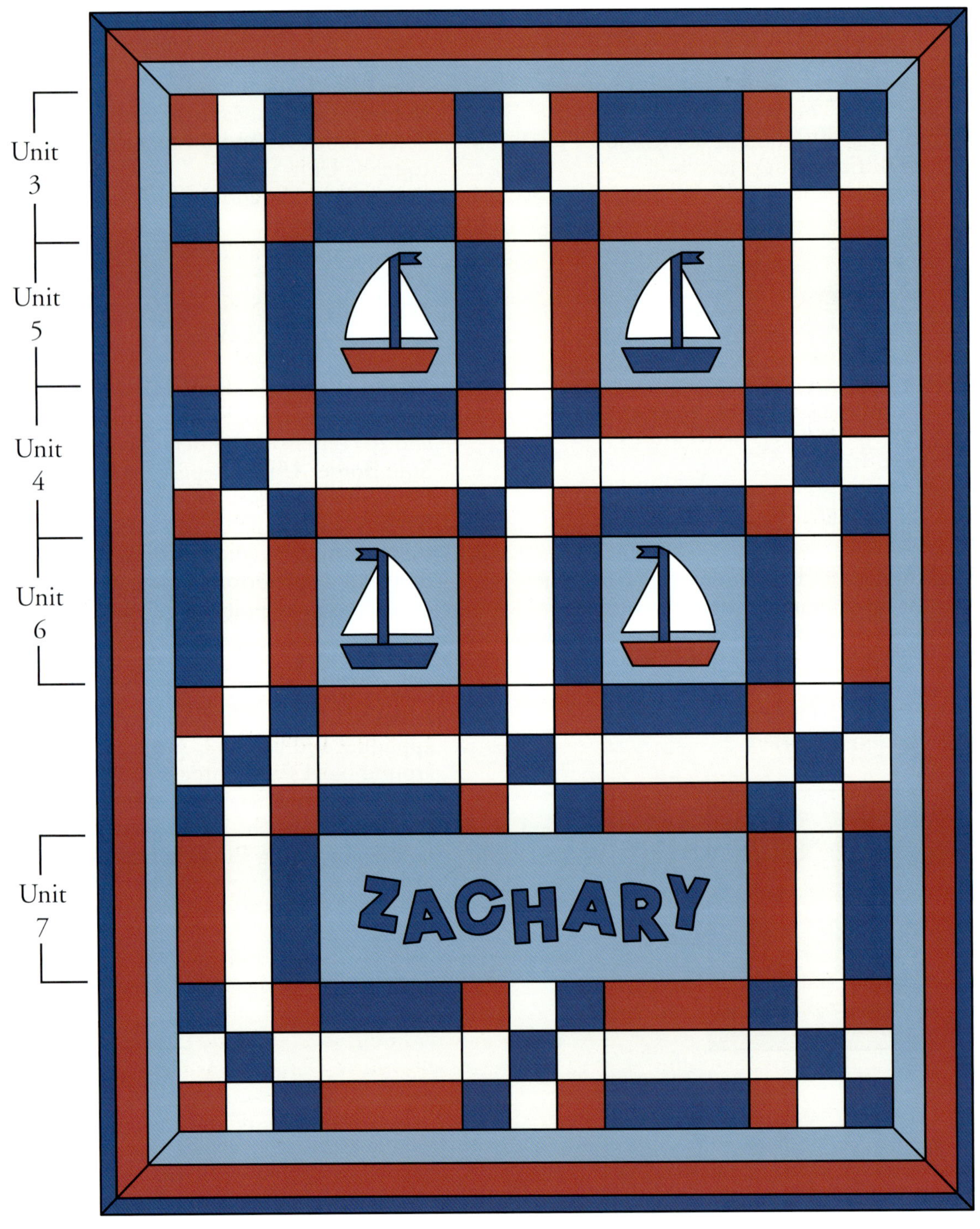

Sailboat Diaper Tote

FABRIC REQUIREMENTS

Yardage is based on 45" (114 cm) wide fabric.
1 yd (91 cm) of fabric for tote and pocket
1 yd (91 cm) **total** of 2 contrasting fabrics for lining and pocket binding and bottom
Scraps of assorted fabrics for sails and appliqués
1 yd (91 cm) of batting

You will also need:
Fusible interfacing
Tracing paper
7" (18 cm) length of grosgrain ribbon 3/8" (.95 cm) wide
1 yd (91 cm) of white rickrack 1/2" (1.3 cm) wide

CUTTING OUT THE PIECES

*Follow **Rotary Cutting**, page 32, to cut fabric. All measurements include a 1/2" seam allowance. Appliqué patterns do not include seam allowances and are reversed. Follow **Preparing Fusible Appliqué Pieces**, page 34, to cut out appliqués from assorted fabrics.*

From tote fabric:

- Cut 2 strips 15" wide. From these strips, cut 1 rectangle 15" x 43" for tote and 1 rectangle 15" x 13" for pocket.

From 2 contrasting fabrics:

- Cut 1 rectangle 15" x 43". Fold in half lengthwise and crosswise and referring to **Fig. 1**, page 29, use **Template**, page 29, to cut tote lining.
- Cut 1 rectangle 15" x 2 1/2" for pocket binding.
- Cut 1 rectangle 15" x 13" for pocket lining.
- Cut 2 rectangles 15" x 3 1/2" for tote bottom.

From assorted fabrics for appliqués:

- Cut 1 boat (**a**).
- Use **Alphabet**, pages 30-31, to cut letters.

From sail fabric:

- Cut 1 sail; cut 1 sail and interfacing in reverse (**f**).
- Cut 1 sail; cut 1 sail and interfacing in reverse (**g**).

From batting:

- Cut 1 rectangle 15" x 43" for tote.
- Cut 1 rectangle 15" x 13" for pocket.

MAKING THE TOTE

*Follow **Piecing** and **Pressing**, page 33, and **Machine Appliqué**, page 34, to make tote. Refer to photo for placement. Use a 1/2" seam allowance for all seams, unless otherwise noted.*

1. Using patterns f and g, page 29, and referring to Sailboat Quilt, Version 2, Block C, Step 1, page 25, make 2 detached sails.
2. Position "AHOY !" and sails on tote pocket, allowing a 1" margin at the top edge and a 3 1/2" margin at the bottom edge. Position ribbon over center of sails. Fold 1 1/2" of ribbon under at top of sails as shown in **Fig. 1**, page 20, and edge stitch in place.

3. Position boat over bottom of ribbon. Fuse letters and boat in place on pocket and appliqué using matching thread and a Satin Stitch.
4. Refer to **Diaper Tote Finishing**, Steps 1-6, page 40, to complete the pocket and baste to tote front. Baste rickrack to pocket and tote back 3¾" from bottom edge.
5. Refer to **Diaper Tote Finishing**, Steps 7-9, page 40, to assemble tote.
6. For squared bottom, match side seams of tote to center bottom seam; sew across each corner 2" from end (**Fig 1**). Repeat for lining.

Fig. 1

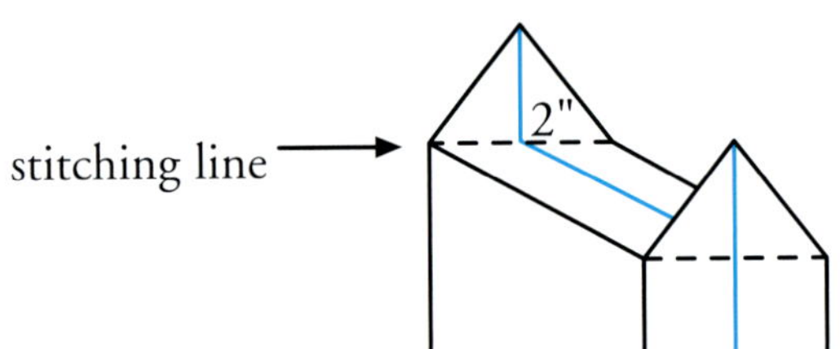

Sailboat Patterns

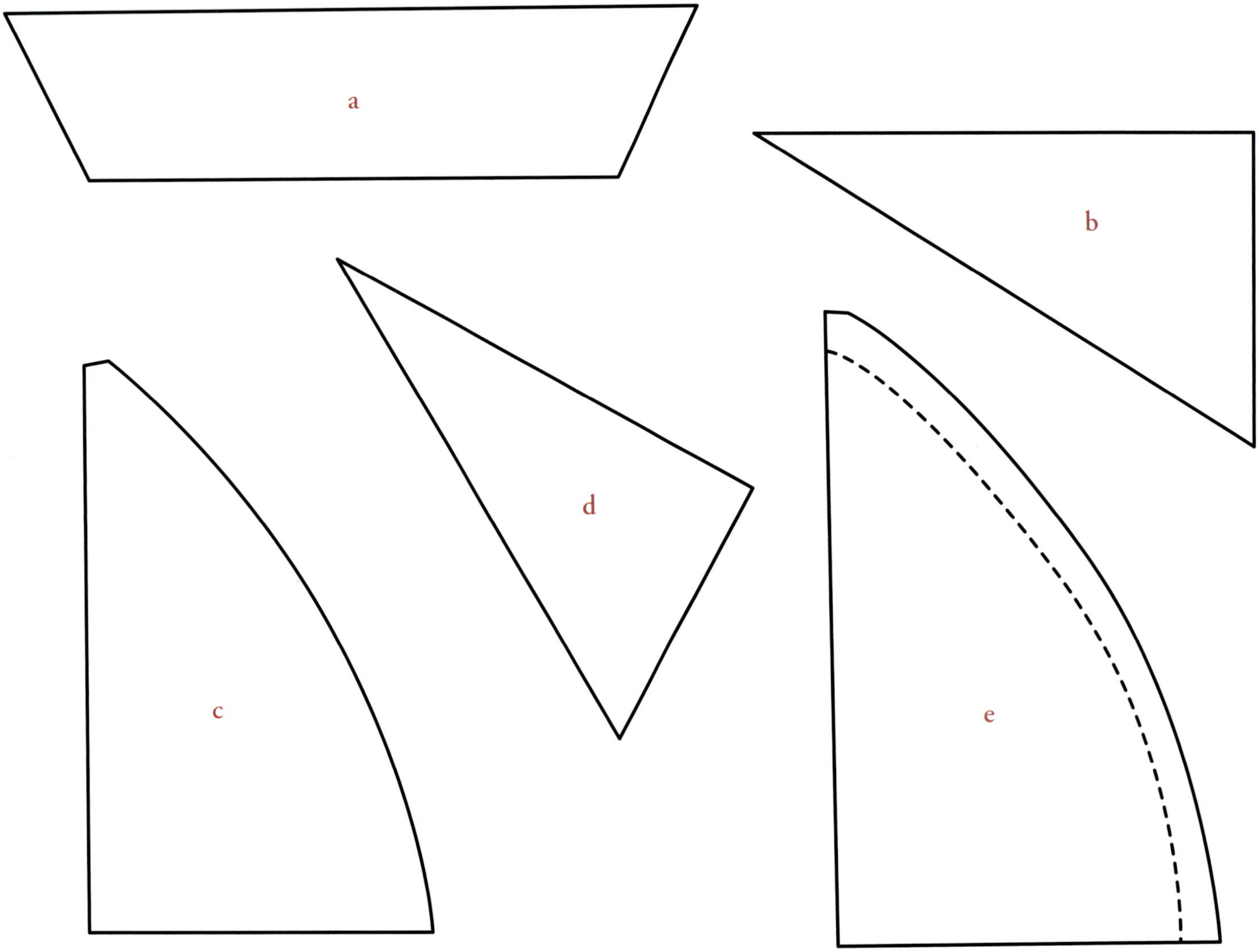

a

b

d

c

e

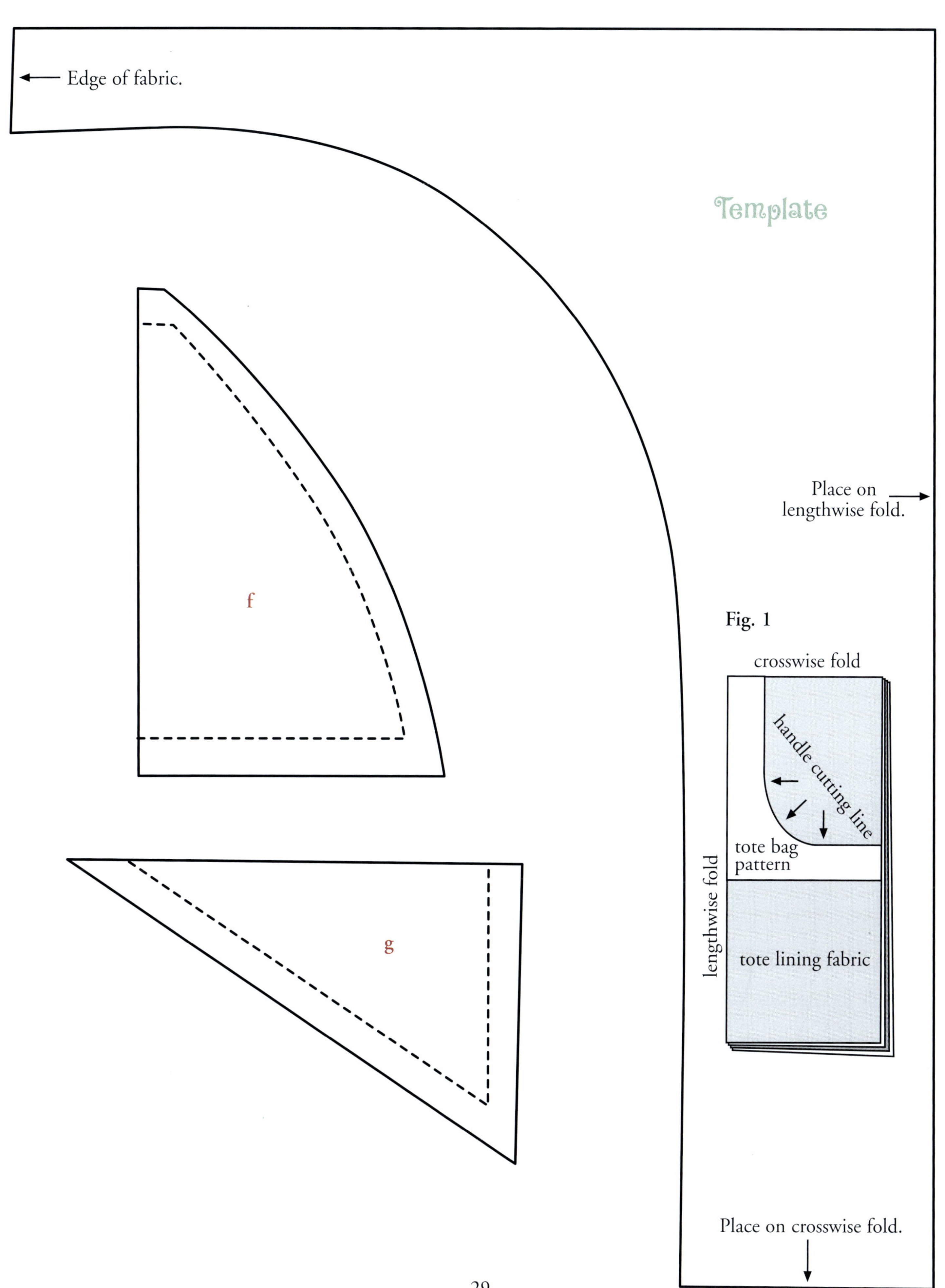
Edge of fabric.
Template
f
g
Place on lengthwise fold.
Fig. 1
crosswise fold
handle cutting line
tote bag pattern
lengthwise fold
tote lining fabric
Place on crosswise fold.

Alphabet Patterns

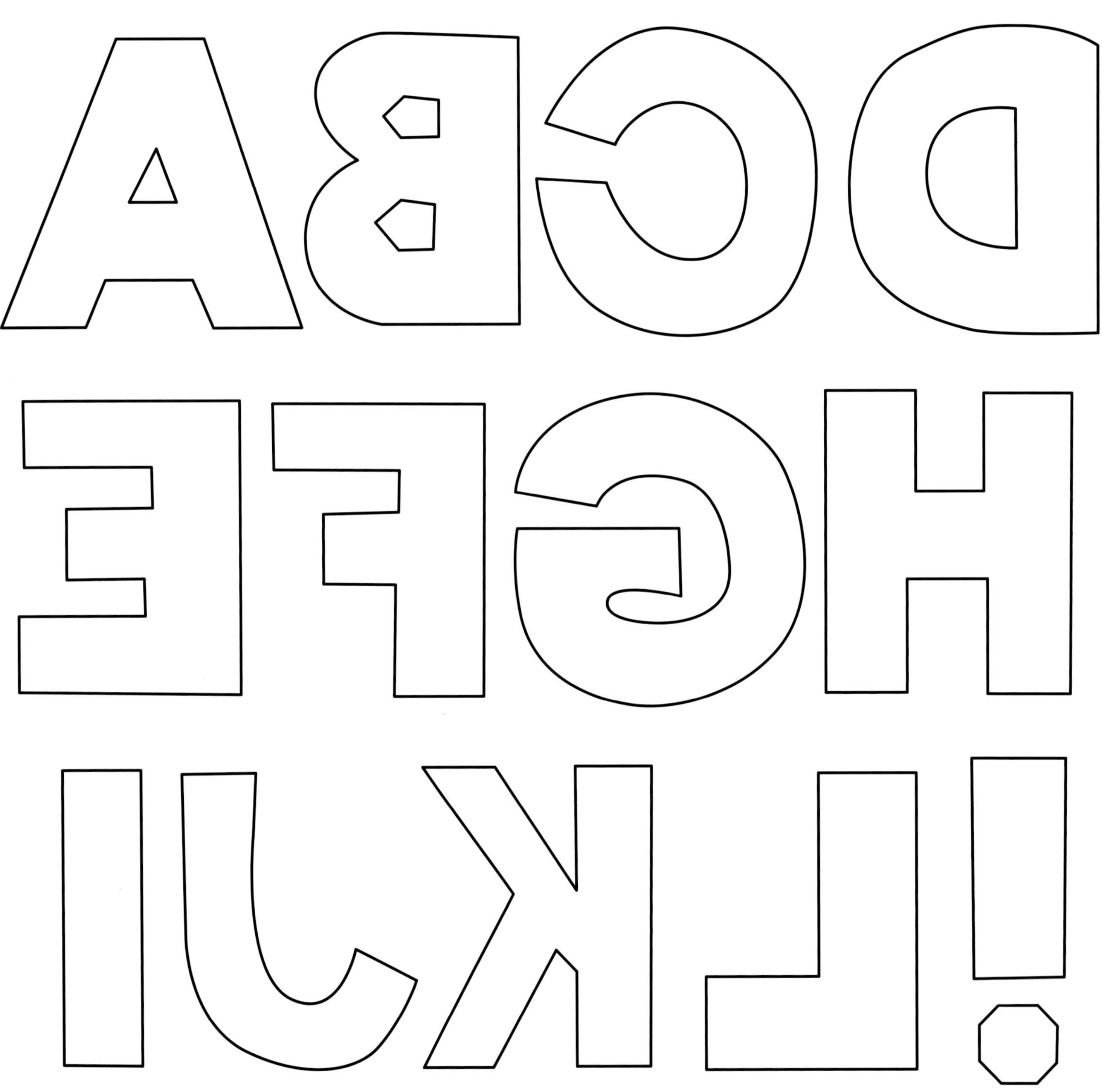

General Instructions

To make your quilting easier and more enjoyable, we encourage you to carefully read all of the general instructions, study the color photographs, and familiarize yourself with the individual project instructions before beginning a project.

Fabrics

SELECTING FABRICS

Choose high-quality, medium-weight 100% cotton fabrics. All-cotton fabrics hold a crease better, fray less, and are easier to quilt than cotton/polyester blends.

Yardage requirements listed for each project are based on 45" wide fabric with a "usable" width of 42" after shrinkage and trimming selvages. Actual usable width will probably vary slightly from fabric to fabric. Our recommended yardage lengths should be adequate for occasional re-squaring of fabric when many cuts are required.

PREPARING FABRICS

We recommend that all fabrics be washed, dried, and pressed before cutting. If fabrics are not pre-washed, washing finished quilt will cause shrinkage and give it a more "antiqued" look and feel. Bright and dark colors, which may run, should always be washed before cutting. After washing and drying fabric, fold lengthwise with wrong sides together and matching selvages.

Rotary Cutting

Rotary cutting has brought speed and accuracy to quiltmaking by allowing quilters to easily cut strips of fabric and then cut those strips into smaller pieces.

- Place fabric on work surface with fold closest to you.
- Cut all strips from selvage-to-selvage width of fabric unless otherwise indicated in project instructions.
- Square left edge of fabric using rotary cutter and rulers (**Figs. 1-2**).

Fig. 1

Fig. 2

- To cut each strip required for a project, place ruler over cut edge of fabric, aligning desired marking on ruler with cut edge; make cut (**Fig. 3**).

Fig. 3

- When cutting several strips from a single piece of fabric, it is important to make sure that cuts remain at a perfect right angle to the fold; square fabric as needed.

Piecing

Precise cutting, followed by accurate piecing, will ensure that all pieces of quilt top fit together well.

HAND PIECING

- Use ruler and sharp fabric marking pencil to draw all seam lines and transfer any alignment markings onto back of cut pieces.
- Matching right sides, pin 2 pieces together, using pins to mark corners.
- Use Running Stitch to sew pieces together along drawn line, backstitching at beginning and end of seam.
- Run 5 or 6 stitches onto needle before pulling needle through fabric.
- To add stability, backstitch every 3/4" to 1".
- Do not extend stitches into seam allowances.

MACHINE PIECING

- Set sewing machine stitch length for approximately 11 stitches per inch.
- Use neutral-colored general-purpose sewing thread (not quilting thread) in needle and in bobbin.
- An accurate 1/4" seam allowance is *essential.* Presser feet that are 1/4" wide are available for most sewing machines.
- When piecing, always place pieces right sides together and match raw edges; pin if necessary.
- Chain piecing saves time and will usually result in more accurate piecing.
- Trim away points of seam allowances that extend beyond edges of sewn pieces.

Sewing Strip Sets

When there are several strips to assemble into a strip set, first sew strips together into pairs, then sew pairs together to form strip set. To help avoid distortion, sew seams in opposite directions (**Fig. 4**).

Fig. 4

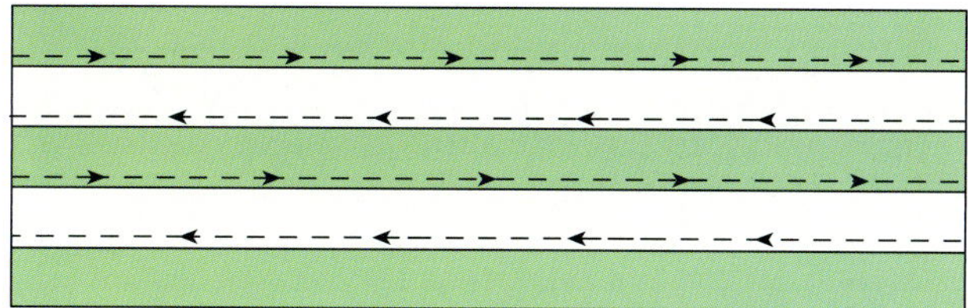

Sewing Across Seam Intersections

When sewing across intersection of 2 seams, place pieces right sides together and match seams exactly, making sure seam allowances are pressed in opposite directions (**Fig. 5**).

Fig. 5

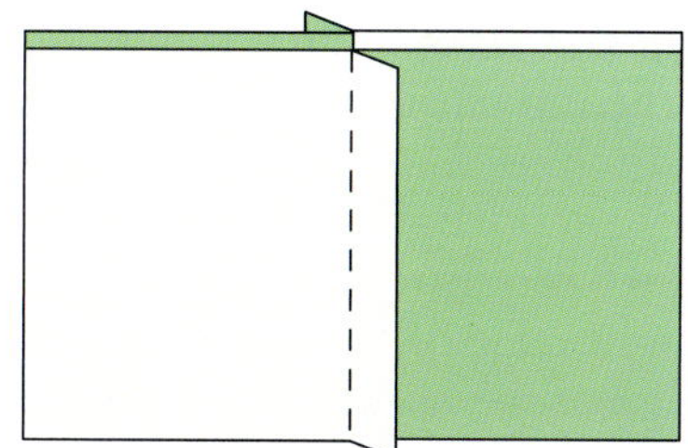

Pressing

- Use steam iron set on "Cotton" for all pressing.
- Press after sewing each seam.
- Seam allowances are almost always pressed to 1 side, usually toward darker fabric. However, to reduce bulk it may occasionally be necessary to press seam allowances toward the lighter fabric or even to press them open.
- To prevent dark fabric seam allowance from showing through light fabric, trim darker seam allowance slightly narrower than lighter seam allowance.
- To press long seams, such as those in long strip sets, without curving or other distortion, lay strips across width of the ironing board.

Machine Appliqué

PREPARING FUSIBLE APPLIQUÉ PIECES

White or light-colored fabrics may need to be lined with fusible interfacing before applying fusible web to prevent darker fabrics from showing through.

1. When using fusible web, appliqué patterns need to be reversed from the way they appear on the finished project. To reverse pattern, trace onto tracing paper and turn paper over.
2. Place paper-backed fusible web, paper side up, over appliqué pattern. Trace pattern onto paper side of web with pencil as many times as indicated in project instructions for a single fabric.
3. Follow manufacturer's instructions to fuse traced patterns to wrong side of fabrics. Do not remove paper backing.
4. Use scissors to cut out appliqué pieces along traced lines. Remove paper backing from all pieces.

SATIN STITCH APPLIQUÉ

A good satin stitch is a thick, smooth, almost solid line of zigzag stitching that covers the exposed raw edges of appliqué pieces.

1. Pin stabilizer, such as paper or any of the commercially available products, on wrong side of background fabric before stitching appliqués in place.
2. Thread sewing machine with general-purpose thread; use general-purpose thread that matches background fabric in bobbin.
3. Set sewing machine for a medium (approximately 1/8") zigzag stitch and a short stitch length. Slightly loosening the top tension may yield a smoother stitch.
4. Begin by stitching 2 or 3 stitches in place (drop feed dogs or set stitch length at 0) to anchor thread. Most of the Satin Stitch should be on the appliqué with the right edge of the stitch falling at the outside edge of the appliqué. Stitch over all exposed raw edges of appliqué pieces.
5. (***Note:*** Dots on **Figs. 6-11** indicate where to leave needle in fabric when pivoting.) For outside corners, stitch just past corner, stopping with needle in background fabric (**Fig. 6**). Raise presser foot. Pivot project, lower presser foot, and stitch adjacent side (**Fig. 7**).

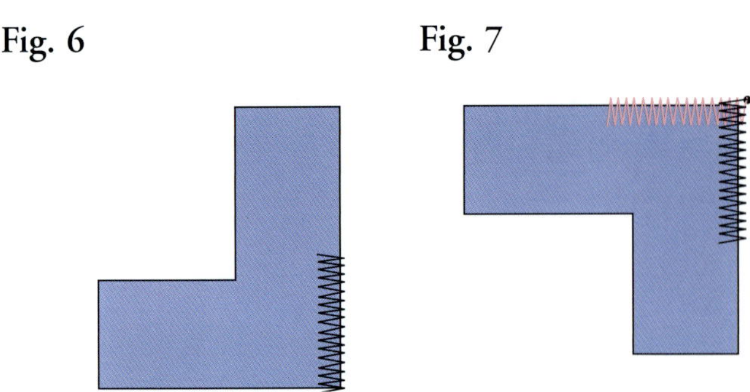

Fig. 6 **Fig. 7**

6. For inside corners, stitch just past corner, stopping with needle in appliqué fabric (**Fig. 8**). Raise presser foot. Pivot project, lower presser foot, and stitch adjacent side (**Fig. 9**).

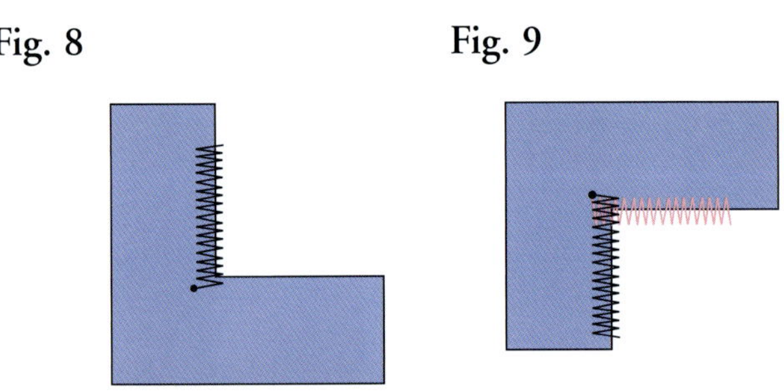

Fig. 8 **Fig. 9**

7. When stitching outside curves, stop with needle in background fabric. Raise presser foot and pivot project as needed. Lower presser foot and continue stitching, pivoting as often as necessary to follow curve (**Fig. 10**).

Fig. 10

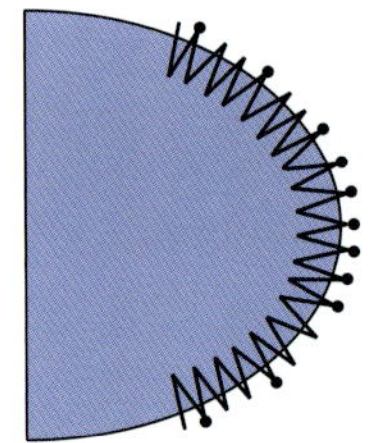

8. When stitching inside curves, stop with needle in appliqué fabric. Raise presser foot and pivot project as needed. Lower presser foot and continue stitching, pivoting as often as necessary to follow curve (**Fig. 11**).

Fig. 11

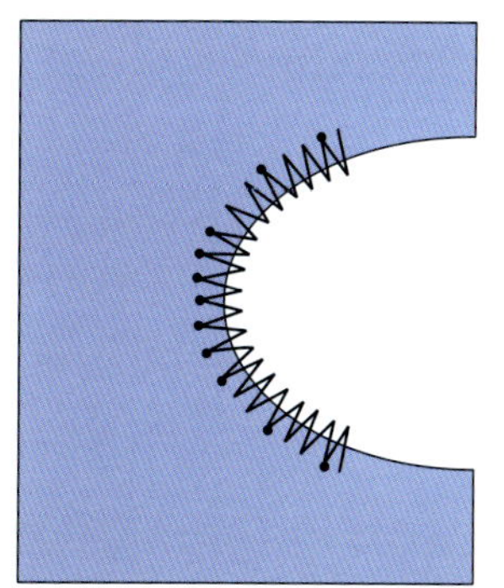

9. Do not backstitch at end of stitching. Pull threads to wrong side of background fabric; knot thread and trim ends.
10. Carefully tear away stabilizer.

DECORATIVE STITCH APPLIQUÉ

Some sewing machines feature a Blanket Stitch similar to the one used in this book. Refer to your Owner's Manual for machine set-up. If your machine does not have this stitch, try any of the decorative stitches your machine has until you are satisfied with the look.

Adding Mitered Borders

1. Mark the center of each edge of quilt top.
2. Mark center of 1 long edge of top border. Measure across center of quilt top. Matching center marks and raw edges, pin border to center of quilt top edge. Beginning at center of border, measure half the width of the quilt top in both directions and mark. Match marks on border with corners of quilt top and pin. Easing in any fullness, pin border to quilt top between center and corners. Sew border to quilt top, beginning and ending seams **exactly** 1/4" from each corner of quilt top and backstitching at beginning and end of stitching (**Fig. 12**).

Fig. 12

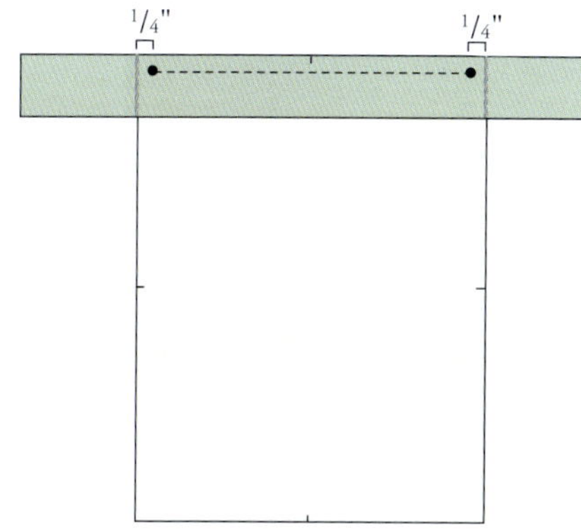

3. Repeat Step 2 to sew bottom, then side borders, to center section of quilt top. To temporarily move first 2 borders out of the way, fold and pin ends as shown in **Fig. 13**.

Fig. 13

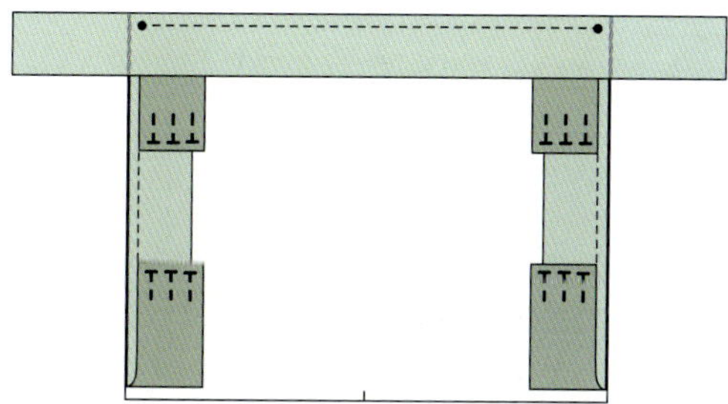

4. Fold 1 corner of quilt top diagonally with right sides together and matching edges. Use ruler to mark stitching line as shown in **Fig. 14**. Pin borders together along drawn line. Sew on drawn line, backstitching at beginning and end of stitching (**Fig. 15**).

Fig. 14

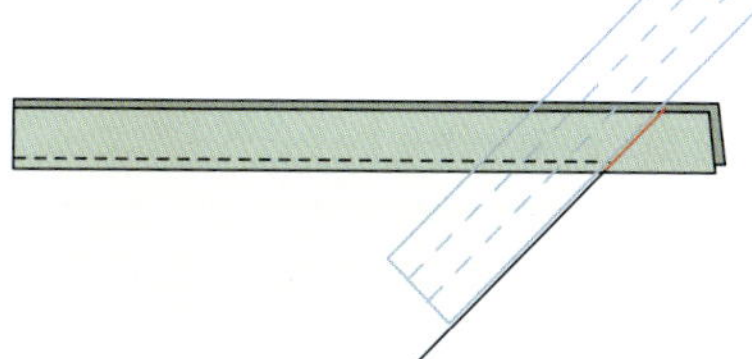

Fig. 15

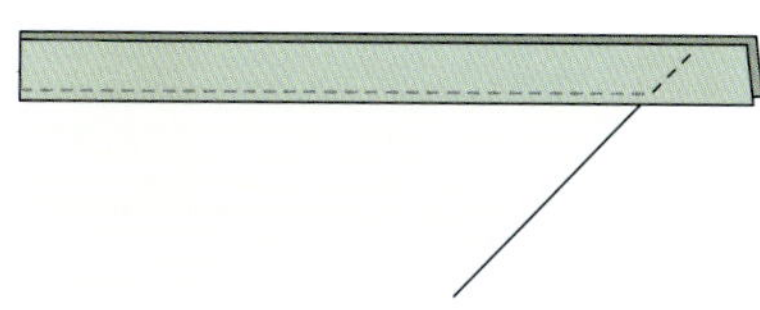

5. Turn mitered corner right side up. Check to make sure corner will lie flat with no gaps or puckers.
6. Trim seam allowance to 1/4"; press to 1 side.
7. Repeat Steps 4-6 to miter each remaining corner.

Quilting

*Quilting holds the 3 layers (top, batting, and backing) of the quilt together and can be done by hand or machine. Because marking, layering, and quilting are interrelated and may be done in different orders depending on circumstances, please read entire **Quilting** section before beginning project.*

TYPES OF QUILTING DESIGNS

In the Ditch Quilting

Quilting along seamlines or along edges of appliquéd pieces is called "in the ditch" quilting. This type of quilting should be done on side **opposite** seam allowance and does not have to be marked.

Outline Quilting

Quilting a consistent distance, usually 1/4", from seam or appliqué is called "outline" quilting. Outline quilting may be marked, or 1/4" masking tape may be placed along seamlines for quilting guide. (Do not leave tape on quilt longer than necessary, since it may leave an adhesive residue.)

MARKING QUILTING LINES

Quilting lines may be marked using fabric marking pencils, chalk markers, water- or air-soluble pens, or lead pencils.

Simple quilting designs may be marked with chalk or chalk pencil after basting. A small area may be marked, then quilted, before moving to next area to be marked. Intricate designs should be marked before basting using a more durable marker.

Caution: Some marks may be permanently set by pressing. **Test** different markers **on scrap fabric** to find one that marks clearly and can be thoroughly removed.

A wide variety of precut quilting stencils, as well as entire books of quilting patterns, are available. Using a stencil makes it easier to mark intricate or repetitive designs.

To make a stencil from a pattern, center template plastic over pattern and use a permanent marker to trace pattern onto plastic. Use a craft knife with single or double blade to cut channels along traced lines (**Fig. 16**).

Fig. 16

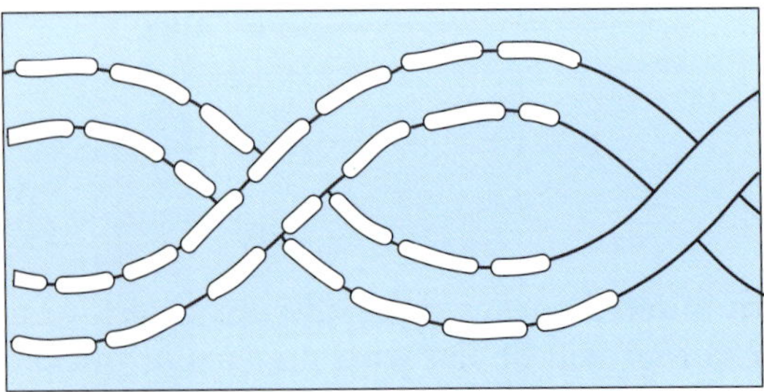

PREPARING THE BACKING

To allow for slight shifting of quilt top during quilting, backing should be approximately 4" larger on all sides. Yardage requirements listed for quilt backings are calculated for 45"w fabric. Using 90"w or 108"w fabric for the backing of a bed-sized quilt may eliminate piecing. To piece a backing using 45"w fabric, use the following instructions.

1. Measure length and width of quilt top; add 8" to each measurement.
2. If determined width is 84" or less, cut backing fabric into 2 lengths slightly longer than determined **length** measurement. Trim selvages. Place lengths with right sides facing and sew long edges together, forming tube (**Fig. 17**). Match seams and press along 1 fold (**Fig. 18**). Cut along pressed fold to form single piece (**Fig. 19**).

Fig. 17 **Fig. 18** **Fig. 19**

3. If determined width is more than 84", cut backing fabric into 3 lengths slightly longer than determined **width** measurement. Trim selvages. Sew long edges together to form single piece.
4. Trim backing to size determined in Step 1; press seam allowances open.

CHOOSING THE BATTING

The appropriate batting will make quilting easier. For fine hand quilting, choose low-loft batting. All cotton or cotton/polyester blend battings work well for machine quilting because the cotton helps "grip" quilt layers. If quilt is to be tied, a high-loft batting, sometimes called extra-loft or fat batting, may be used to make quilt "fluffy."

Types of batting include cotton, polyester, cotton/polyester blend, wool, cotton/wool blend, and silk.

When selecting batting, refer to package labels for characteristics and care instructions. Cut batting same size as prepared backing.

ASSEMBLING THE QUILT

1. Examine wrong side of quilt top closely; trim any seam allowances and clip any threads that may show through front of the quilt. Press quilt top, being careful not to "set" any marked quilting lines.
2. Place backing **wrong** side up on flat surface. Use masking tape to tape edges of backing to surface. Place batting on top of backing fabric. Smooth batting gently, being careful not to stretch or tear. Center quilt top **right** side up on batting.
3. If hand quilting, begin in center and work toward outer edges to hand baste all layers together. Use long stitches and place basting lines approximately 4" apart (**Fig. 20**). Smooth fullness or wrinkles toward outer edges.

Fig. 20

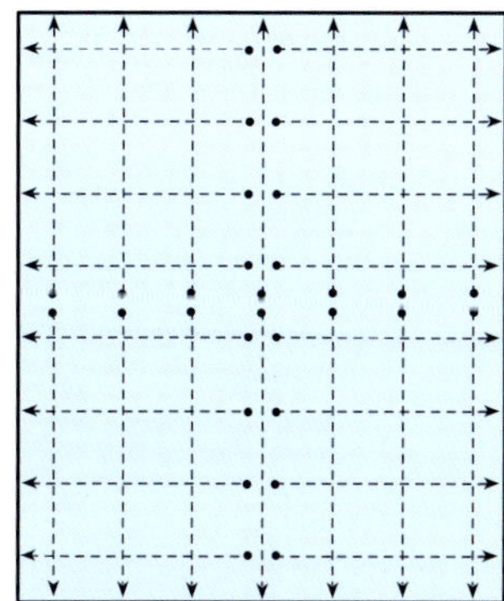

4. If machine quilting, use 1" rustproof safety pins to "pin-baste" all layers together, spacing pins approximately 4" apart. Begin at center and work toward outer edges to secure all layers. If possible, place pins away from areas that will be quilted, although pins may be removed as needed when quilting.

HAND QUILTING

The quilting stitch is a basic running stitch that forms a broken line on quilt top and backing. Stitches on quilt top and backing should be straight and equal in length.

1. Secure center of quilt in hoop or frame. Check quilt top and backing to make sure they are smooth. To help prevent puckers, always begin quilting in the center of quilt and work toward outside edges.
2. Thread needle with 18" - 20" length of quilting thread; knot 1 end. Using thimble, insert needle into quilt top and batting approximately 1/2" from quilting line. Bring needle up on quilting line (**Fig. 21**); when knot catches on quilt top, give thread a quick, short pull to "pop" knot through fabric into batting (**Fig. 22**).

Fig. 21

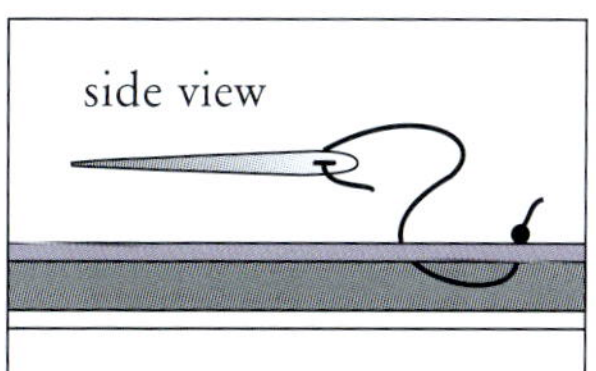

Fig. 22

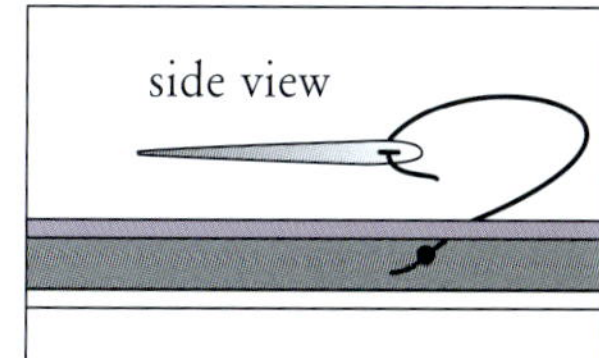

3. Holding needle with sewing hand and placing other hand underneath quilt, use thimble to push tip of needle down through all layers. As soon as needle touches finger underneath, use that finger to push tip of needle only back up through layers to top of quilt. (The amount of needle showing above fabric determines length of quilting stitch.) Referring to **Fig. 23**, rock needle up and down, taking 3 - 6 stitches before bringing needle and thread completely through layers. Check back of quilt to make sure stitches are going through all layers. If necessary, make 1 stitch at a time when quilting through seam allowances or along curves and corners.

Fig. 23

4. At end of thread, knot thread close to fabric and "pop" knot into batting; clip thread close to fabric.
5. Move hoop as often as necessary. Thread may be left dangling and picked up again after returning to that part of quilt.

MACHINE QUILTING METHODS

Use general-purpose thread in bobbin. Do not use quilting thread. Thread the needle of machine with general-purpose thread or transparent monofilament thread to make quilting blend with quilt top fabrics. Use decorative thread, such as a metallic or contrasting-color general-purpose thread, to make quilting lines stand out more.

Straight Line Quilting

The term "straight-line" is somewhat deceptive, since curves (especially gentle ones) as well as straight lines can be stitched with this technique.

1. Set stitch length for 6 - 10 stitches per inch and attach walking foot to sewing machine.
2. Determine which section of quilt will have longest continuous quilting line, oftentimes area from center top to center bottom. Roll up and secure each edge of quilt to help reduce the bulk, keeping fabrics smooth. Smaller projects may not need to be rolled.
3. Begin stitching on longest quilting line, using very short stitches for the first 1/4" to "lock" quilting. Stitch across project, using 1 hand on each side of walking foot to slightly spread fabric and to guide fabric through machine. Lock stitches at end of quilting line.
4. Continue machine quilting, stitching longer quilting lines first to stabilize quilt before moving on to other areas.

Binding

Binding encloses the raw edges of quilt. Because of its stretchiness, bias binding works well for binding projects with curves or rounded corners and tends to lie smooth and flat in any given circumstance. Binding may also be cut from straight lengthwise or crosswise grain of fabric.

MAKING STRAIGHT-GRAIN BINDING

1. Cut lengthwise or crosswise strips of binding fabric the determined length and the width called for in project instructions. Piece strips to achieve necessary length.
2. Matching wrong sides and raw edges, press strip(s) in half lengthwise to complete binding.

ATTACHING BINDING WITH MITERED CORNERS

1. Beginning with 1 end near center on bottom edge of quilt, lay binding around quilt to make sure that seams in binding will not end up at a corner. Adjust placement if necessary. Matching raw edges of binding to raw edge of quilt top, pin binding to right side of quilt along 1 edge.
2. When you reach first corner, mark 1/4" from corner of quilt top (**Fig. 24**).

Fig. 24

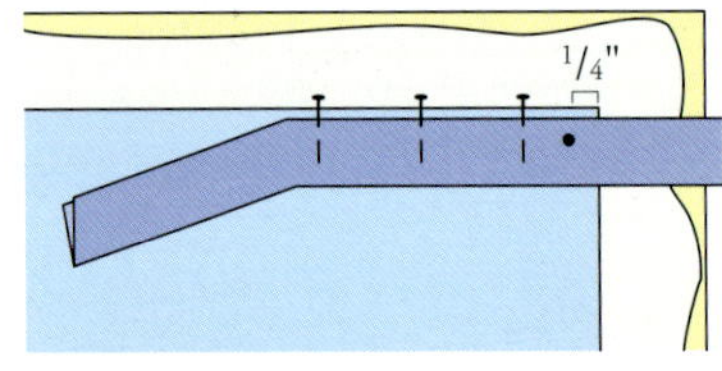

3. Beginning approximately 10" from end of binding and using 1/4" seam allowance, sew binding to quilt, backstitching at beginning of stitching and at mark (**Fig. 25**). Lift needle out of fabric and clip thread.

Fig. 25

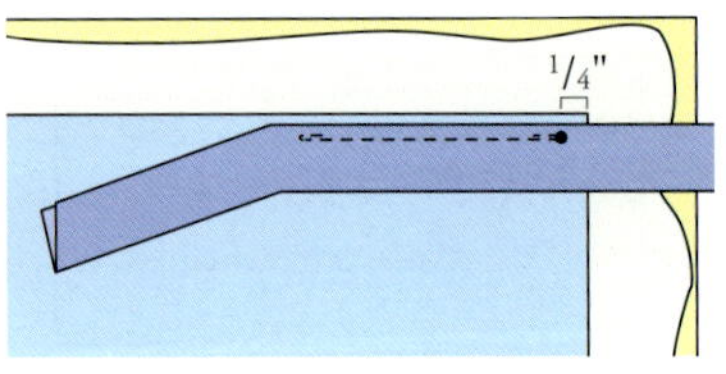

4. Fold binding as shown in **Figs. 26-27** and pin binding to adjacent side, matching raw edges. When reaching the next corner, mark 1/4" from edge of quilt top.

Fig. 26

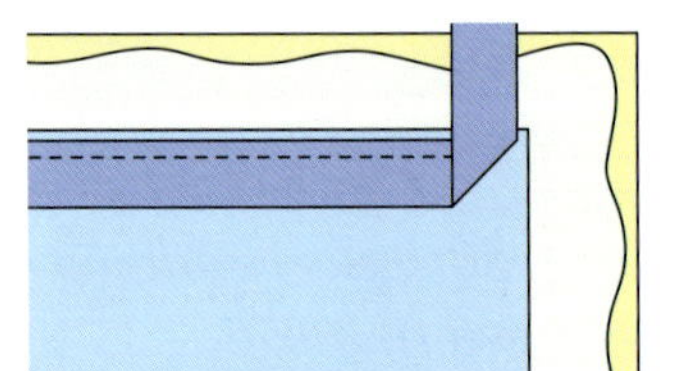

Fig. 27

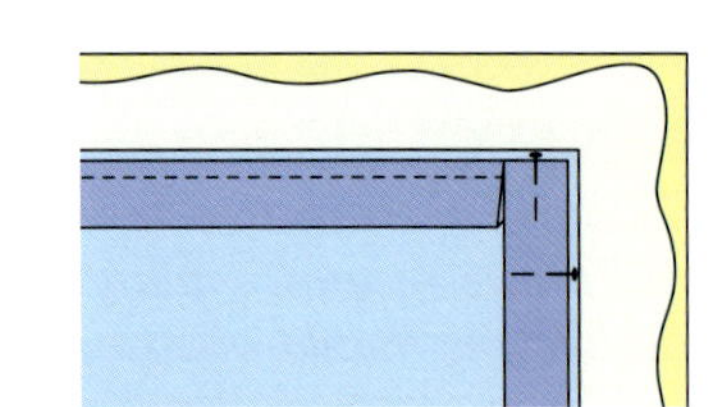

5. Backstitching at edge of quilt top, sew pinned binding to quilt (**Fig. 28**); backstitch at the next mark. Lift needle out of fabric and clip thread.

Fig. 28

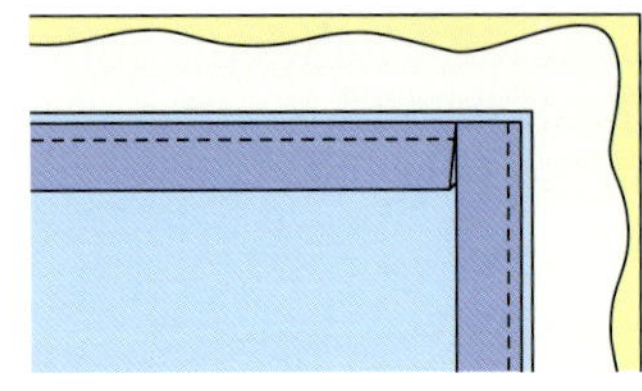

6. Continue sewing binding to quilt, stopping approximately 10" from starting point (**Fig. 29**).

Fig. 29

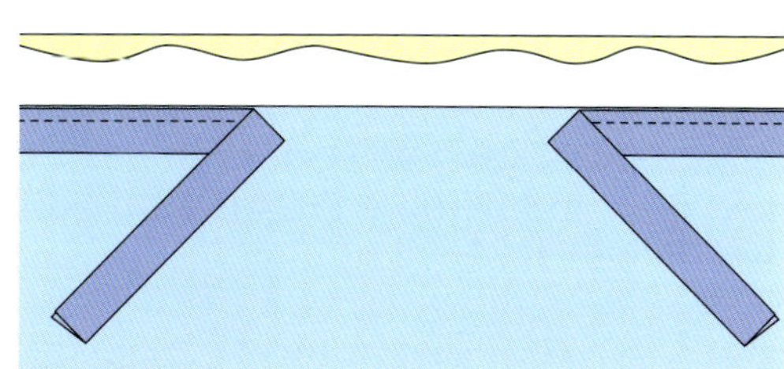

7. Bring beginning and end of binding to center of opening and fold each end back, leaving a 1/4" space between folds (**Fig. 30**). Finger-press folds.

Fig. 30

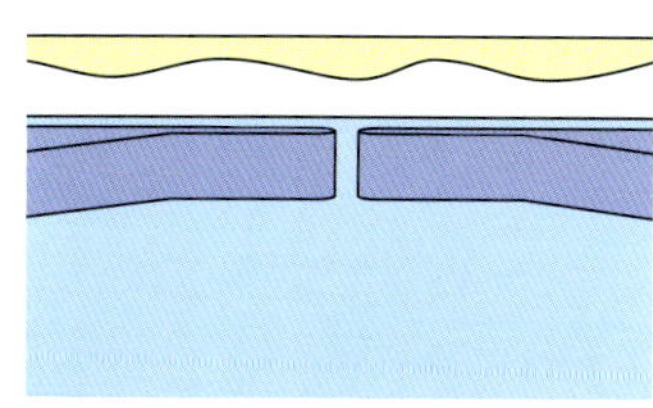

8. Unfold ends of binding and draw a line across wrong side in finger-pressed crease. Draw a line through the lengthwise pressed fold of binding at same spot to create a cross mark. With edge of ruler at marked cross, line up 45° angle marking on ruler with one long side of binding. Draw a diagonal line from edge to edge. Repeat on remaining end, making sure that the two lines are angled the same way (**Fig. 31**).

Fig. 31

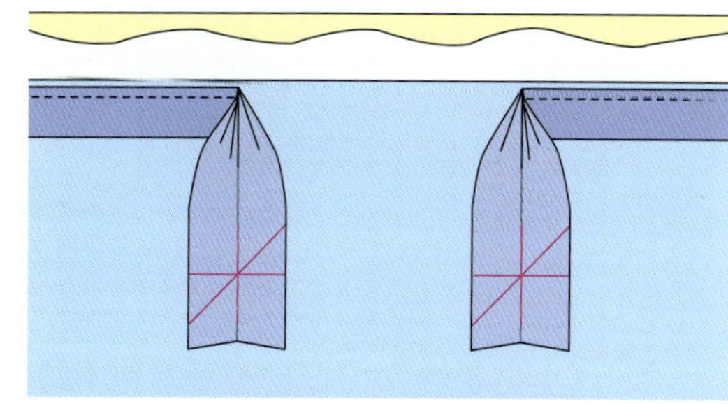

9. Matching right sides and diagonal lines, pin binding ends together at right angles (**Fig. 32**).

Fig. 32

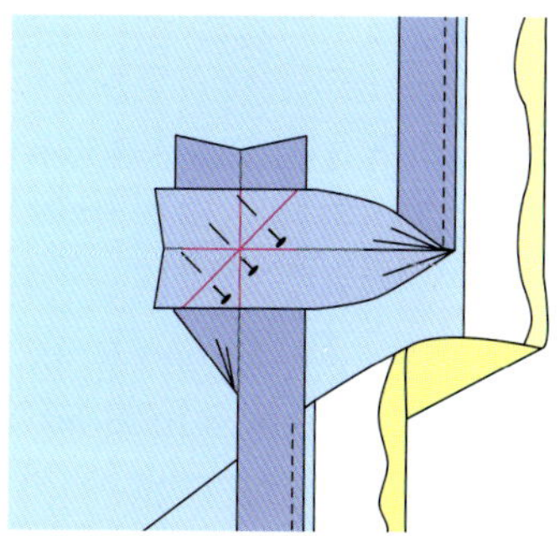

10. Machine stitch along diagonal line, removing pins as you stitch (**Fig. 33**).

Fig. 33

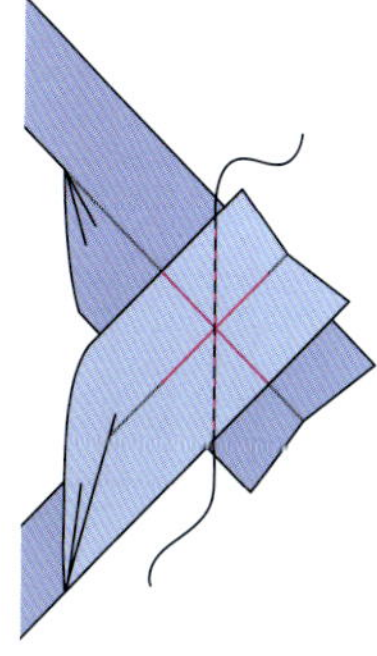

11. Lay binding against quilt to double-check that it is correct length.
12. Trim binding ends, leaving 1/4" seam allowance; press seam open. Stitch binding to quilt.
13. If using 2 1/2"w binding (finished size 1/2"), trim backing and batting a scant 1/4" larger than quilt top so that batting and backing will fill the binding when it is folded over to quilt backing.
14. On 1 edge of quilt, fold binding over to quilt backing and pin pressed edge in place, covering stitching line (**Fig. 34**). On adjacent side, fold binding over, forming a mitered corner (**Fig. 35**). Repeat to pin remainder of binding in place.

Fig. 34

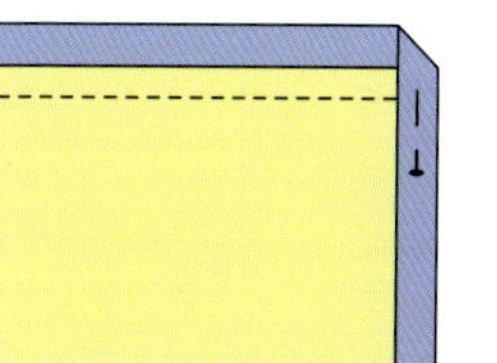

Fig. 35

15. Blindstitch binding to backing, taking care not to stitch through to front of quilt.

Diaper Tote Finishing

Use a 1/2" seam allowance unless otherwise noted.

1. Layer pocket lining (right side down), pocket batting, and appliquéd pocket (right side up) together and quilt as desired.
2. Baste close to raw edges.
3. Turn one long edge of pocket binding 1/2" to wrong side and press. Matching right sides and long edges, sew pocket binding to top edge of pocket. Fold binding to wrong side of pocket and blindstitch in place.
4. Layer tote batting, tote rectangle (right side up), and tote lining (right side down) together and pin in place.
5. Sew around tote handles as shown in **Fig. 36**. Trim seam allowances through all 3 layers. Clip curves and turn right side out.

Fig. 36

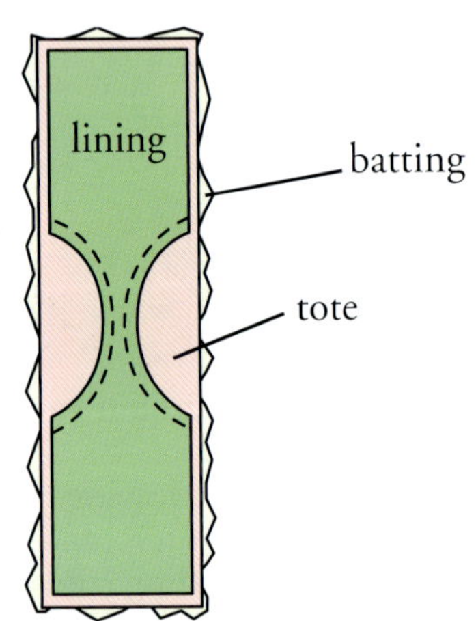

6. With lining pulled out of the way, position pocket on tote front. Top of pocket should be 1/2" below handle seam (**Fig. 37**). Baste pocket in place.

Fig. 37

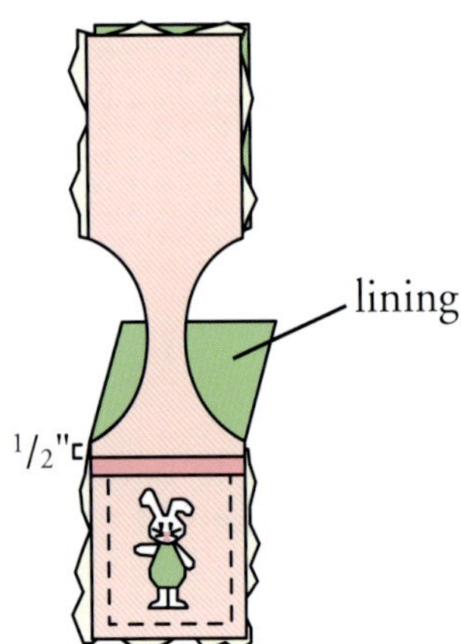

7. With right sides together and lining pulled out of the way, position one long edge of tote bottom 3 1/4" from bottom edge of pocket (**Fig. 38**). Using a 1/4" seam allowance, sew tote bottom to pocket through pocket, tote, and batting. Press toward bottom of pocket. Repeat for back of tote.

Fig. 38

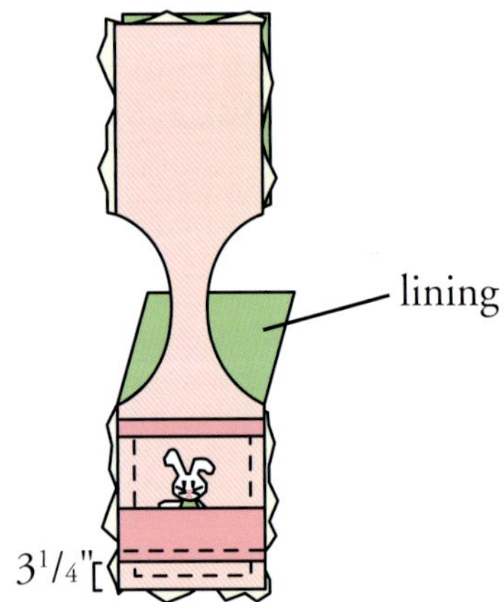

8. Matching right sides, raw edges, and seams, pin tote front and back and lining pieces together. Leaving an opening for turning at bottom of lining, sew sections together (**Fig. 39**).

Fig. 39

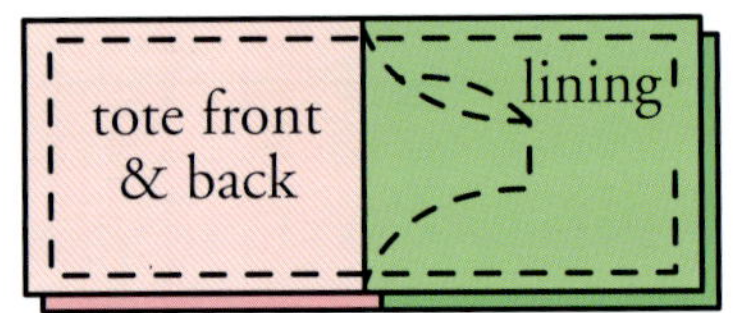

BLANKET STITCH

Come up at 1, go down at 2, and come up at 3, keeping thread below point of needle (**Fig. 40**). Continue working as shown in **Fig. 41**.

Fig. 40

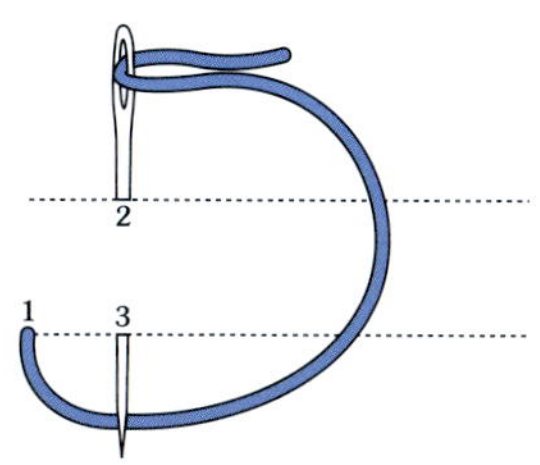

Fig. 41

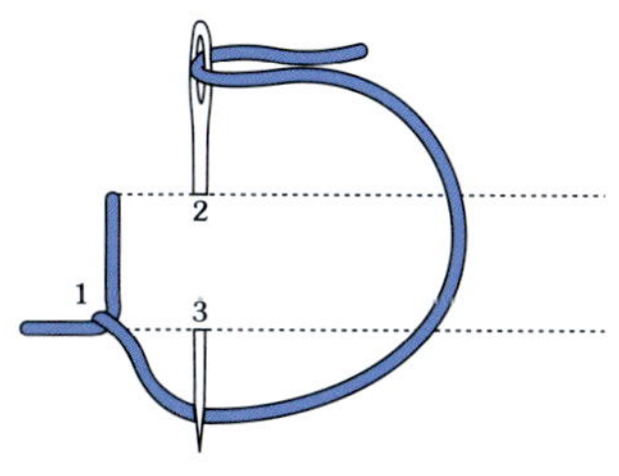

BLIND STITCH

Come up at 1, go down at 2, and come up at 3 (**Fig. 42**). Length of stitches may be varied as desired.

Fig. 42

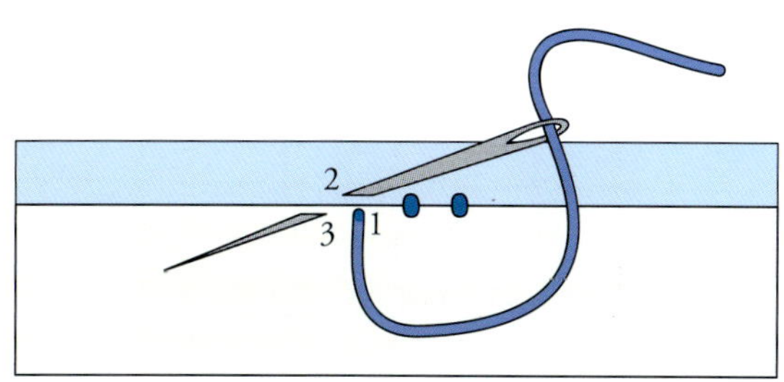

FRENCH KNOT

Follow **Figs. 43-46** to complete French Knots. Come up at 1. Wrap thread twice around needle and insert needle at 2, holding end of thread with non-stitching fingers. Tighten knot then pull needle through, holding floss until it must be released.

Fig. 43

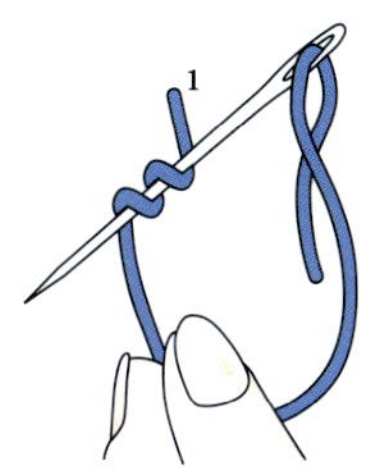

Fig. 44

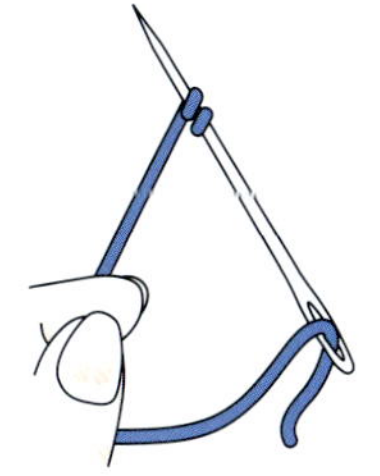

Fig. 45

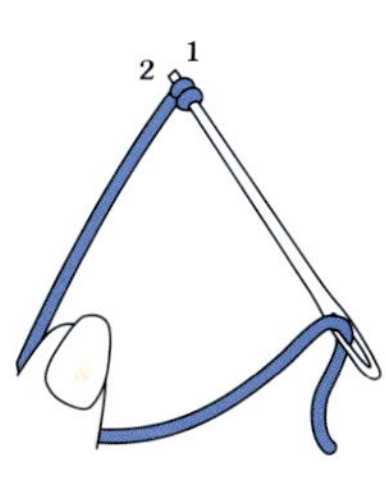

Fig. 46

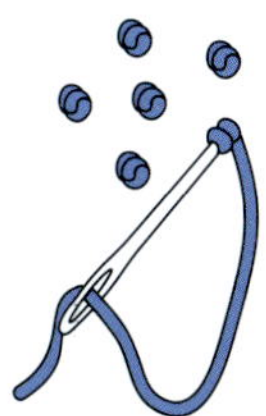

LAZY DAISY STITCH

Come up at 1 and go down again at 1 to form a loop. Come up at 2. Keeping loop below point of needle (**Fig. 47**), go down at 3 to anchor loop (**Fig. 48**).

Fig. 47

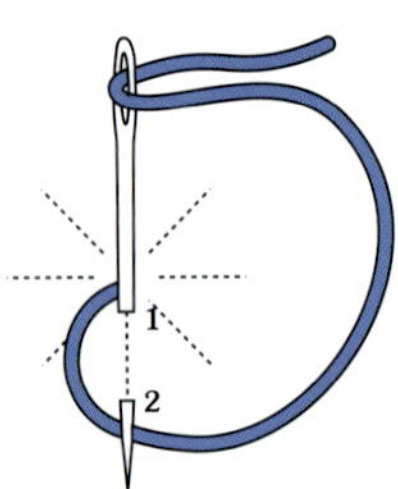

Fig. 48

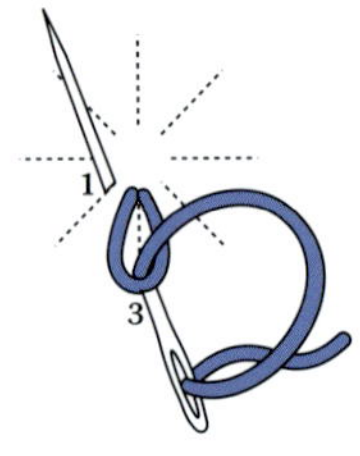

STEM STITCH

Come up at 1. Keeping thread below the stitching line, go down at 2 and come up at 3. Go down at 4 and come up at 5 (**Fig. 49**).

Fig. 49

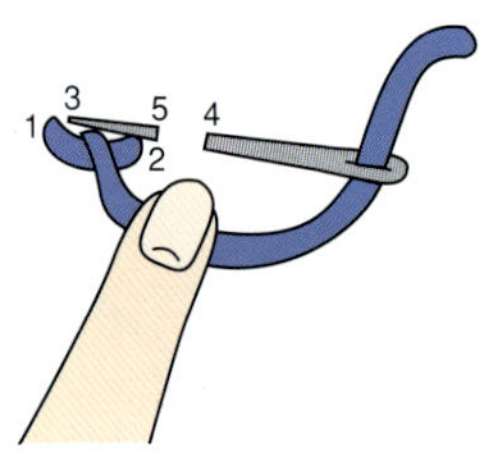

STRAIGHT STITCH

Come up at 1 and go down at 2 (**Fig. 50**). Length of stitches may be varied as desired.

Fig. 50

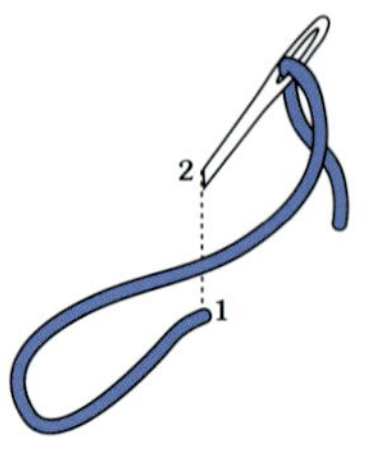

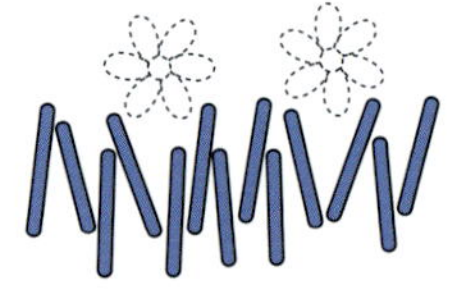

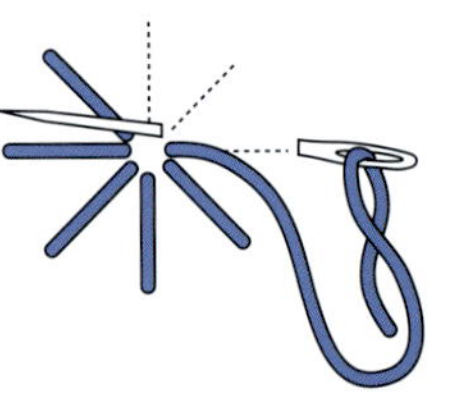

Signing and Dating Your Quilt

A completed quilt is a work of art and should be signed and dated. There are many different ways to do this and numerous books on the subject. The label should reflect the style of the quilt, the occasion or person for which it was made, and the quilter's own particular talents. Following are suggestions for recording the history of the quilt or adding a sentiment for future generations.

- Embroider quilter's name, date, and any additional information on quilt top or backing. Matching floss, such as cream floss on white border, will leave a subtle record. Bright or contrasting floss will make the information stand out.
- Make label from muslin and use permanent marker to write information. Use different colored permanent markers to make label more decorative. Stitch label to back of quilt.
- Use photo-transfer paper to add image to white or cream fabric label. Stitch label to back of quilt.
- Piece an extra block from quilt top pattern to use as label. Add information with permanent fabric pen. Appliqué block to back of quilt.
- Write message on appliquéd design from quilt top. Attach appliqué to back of the quilt.

Metric Conversion Chart

Metric Conversion Chart

Inches x 2.54 = centimeters (cm)	Yards x .9144 = meters (m)
Inches x 25.4 = millimeters (mm)	Yards x 91.44 = centimeters (cm)
Inches x .0254 = meters (m)	Centimeters x .3937 = inches (")
	Meters x 1.0936 = yards (yd)

Standard Equivalents

1/8"	3.2 mm	0.32 cm	1/8 yard	11.43 cm	0.11 m
1/4"	6.35 mm	0.635 cm	1/4 yard	22.86 cm	0.23 m
3/8"	9.5 mm	0.95 cm	3/8 yard	34.29 cm	0.34 m
1/2"	12.7 mm	1.27 cm	1/2 yard	45.72 cm	0.46 m
5/8"	15.9 mm	1.59 cm	5/8 yard	57.15 cm	0.57 m
3/4"	19.1 mm	1.91 cm	3/4 yard	68.58 cm	0.69 m
7/8"	22.2 mm	2.22 cm	7/8 yard	80 cm	0.8 m
1 "	25.4 mm	2.54 cm	1 yard	91.44 cm	0.91 m

Production Team: Technical Writer - Andrea Ahlen; Editorial Writer - Kimberly L. Ross; Graphic Artists - Amy Gerke and Chad Brown; Photography Stylist - Sondra Daniel

ISBN 1-57486-665-6

Notes